Simon Step

Blindsi

with an introduction by Jacqueline Bolton

Bloomsbury Methuen Drama
An imprint of Bloomsbury Publishing Plc

B L O O M S B U R Y

LONDON · OXFORD · NEW YORK · NEW DELHI · SYDNEY

Bloomsbury Methuen Drama
An imprint of Bloomsbury Publishing Plc

Imprint previously known as Methuen Drama

50 Bedford Square	1385 Broadway
London	New York
WC1B 3DP	NY 10018
UK	USA

www.bloomsbury.com

BLOOMSBURY, METHUEN DRAMA and the Diana logo are trademarks of Bloomsbury Publishing Plc

First published in 2014
Reprinted 2015, 2016

British Library Cataloguing-in-Publication Data
A catalogue record for this book is available from the British Library.

ISBN: PB: 978-1-4725-6871-7
ePDF: 978-1-4725-6869-4
ePUB: 978-1-4725-6870-0

Library of Congress Cataloging-in-Publication Data
A catalog record for this book is available from the Library of Congress.

Series: Modern Plays

Typeset by Mark Heslington Ltd, Scarborough, North Yorkshire
Printed and bound in Great Britain

Introduction

Blindsided is Simon Stephens's fourth play for the Royal
Exchange Theatre, Manchester, following upon the
successes of *Port* (2002, winner of the Pearson Award for Best
New Play), *On the Shore of the Wide World* (2005, winner of the
Olivier Award for Best New Play) and *Punk Rock* (2009,
nominated for the Theatre Management Association Award
for Best New Play). All four plays are set, and emotionally
rooted in, the sights, sounds, smells and shapes of buildings,
roads, heaths, bus stations, parks and town centres located in
and around Stockport, where Stephens was born and grew
up. Three of these plays – *Port*, *On the Shore of the Wide World*
and now *Blindsided* – depict three generations of the same
family, and two – *Port* and *Blindsided* - feature a female
protagonist (interestingly, to date, Stephens's only other play
to visit Stockport, *Harper Regan* (2008), also features three
generations of family and a female protagonist). Family,
history and geography are, in these plays, inextricable from
one another, sparking epic, domestic dramas of love,
violence, regret and compassion.

  In *Blindsided*, Stephens returns to a central preoccupation
within his work, starkly articulated by the playwright as 'the
terrified possibility of acts of random violence'.[1] Previous
plays have evidenced a brooding concern with the sudden
death of young children, refracted here through what
Stephens describes as part of 'Manchester folklore':[2] the
Moors Murders. *Blindsided* is set in Reddish, Greater
Manchester, situated two miles out of Stockport and between
Gorton, Ashton-under-Lyne and Longsight: towns from
which, between July 1963 and October 1965, five children
aged between ten and seventeen were abducted, murdered
and buried in shallow graves on Saddleworth Moor. The

---

[1] Simon Stephens, Introduction to *Plays One* (London: Methuen Drama,
2005), p. xi.
[2] Simon Stephens, personal correspondence with Jacqueline Bolton, 19
December 2013. All further quotations, unless otherwise attributed, are
taken from this source.

murders were committed by a local young couple: Ian Brady and Myra Hindley.[3] The actions and passions of Brady and Hindley, as lovers, as conspirators and as murderers, stretch long shadows over *Blindsided*:

John   I can always find something to explore, me. Always find somewhere to go. Something to do. Someone to play with. We wouldn't have to bring little Spazzy Bones with us would we? Sorry. That's just an affectionate little nickname I just made up for her just now this second. Was it really horrible? You know I don't mean it. I've rather taken to her. I have, Cathy. Do you forgive me? Cathy, please will you forgive me for calling Ruthy 'spazzy bones' and suggesting we leave her here in the middle of the Vale?[4]

Stephens describes *Blindsided* as a kind of 'fantasy, a nightmare' in which he explores 'the destructive, murderous consequences of falling in love with the wrong person'. The suddenness, randomness and absoluteness of Cathy Heyer's love for John Connolly is, at one and the same time, risible, disturbing and compelling:

Cathy   [. . .] I love this feeling.

They lie there for some time.

I feel like every bit of me is awake and asleep at the same time.

They lie there for some time.

---

[3] Brady and Hindley were given life sentences for the murders of Edward Evans (17), Lesley Anne Downey (10) and John Kilbride (12), and were suspected – and later convicted – of the murders of Pauline Reade (16) and Keith Bennett (12). Downey and Reade had been discovered in shallow graves on Saddleworth Moor but it wasn't until 1987 that Pauline Reade's body was also discovered there; to this day Bennett's body remains undiscovered.

[4] Simon Stephens, *Blindsided* (London: Methuen Drama, 2014), p. 26. All page numbers in brackets are taken from this source.

[. . .] When I'm with you. I don't worry about all the things that have happened to me. And I don't worry about the things that are going to happen to me. I don't worry about Ruthy. I feel like I'm kind of just there.

John   I've known you three days Cathy.

Cathy   I can get rather attached to people quite suddenly. (p. 12)

Susan Heyer, aged roughly 37 in 1979 when the play opens, represents a generation whose early twenties were shaped by images of and, moreover, proximity to the Moors Murders. Her bitter suspicion of John Connolly is matched by her frightened protectiveness over both Cathy and Ruthy Heyer: 'there is no way John Connolly is looking after my grand-daughter' (p. 53). Susan's confrontation with John is charged with the fear of his influence over her daughter:

Susan   Don't you dare think you're taking her away from me because you're really not going to do that.

[. . .]

You don't frighten me. You're a little boy.

John   That girl would do anything I told her to.

Susan   She fucking wouldn't.

John   You want to try me?

Pause. (p. 32)

Contrary to what the play invites us to contemplate, however, the horror at the heart of the play lies elsewhere; not in the murderous conspiracy of lovers but in a singular act of vengeance. The killing of a child in order to revenge a disloyal lover is, of course, an image lifted directly from Euripides' *Medea*, itself a meditation upon a classical Greek myth. Discovering that her husband, Jason of the Argonauts, has upon their return to Greece taken King Creon's daughter as a new wife, Medea resolves to avenge his betrayal by killing their own children:

> [. . .] I shall kill my own children.
> My children, there is none who can give them safety.
> And when I have ruined the whole of Jason's house,
> I shall leave the land and flee from the murder of my
> Dear children, and I shall have done a dreadful deed.
> For it is not bearable to be mocked by enemies.
> So it must happen. What profit have I in life?
> I have no land, no home, no refuge from my pain.
> My mistake was made the time I left behind me
> My father's house, and trusted the words of a Greek,
> Who, with heaven's help, will pay me the price for that.[5]

Medea's instincts are chillingly echoed by Cathy in her response to Susan's plea for her to leave John and return to the home which, like Medea, Cathy rejected in favour of her lover:

Cathy I'd look pretty stupid if I did though wouldn't I? It has to be a bit more than that doesn't it.

Susan What do you mean?

Cathy I can't just let him get away with treating me like this and just come home and pretend it never happened.

Susan What are you talking about?

Cathy I'm going to have to do something a bit more than that Mum, don't you think? (p. 58)

In both Cathy and Medea we see the devastating fallout of a 'heart on fire with passionate love'.[6] Dramaturgically, both plays anticipate the dreadful act. Where Euripides' chorus warn that they fear Medea's 'violent heart' and have 'seen

---

[5] Euripides, *Medea*, trans. Rex Warner (New York: Dover Publications, 1993), p. 26.
[6] Ibid., p. 1.

her already blazing her eyes at [her children]',[7] Cathy's bright, upbeat conversation with Isaac Berg, as she pushes Ruthy's buggy, in retrospect signals with unnerving transparency the violence for which her heart is preparing:

Isaac He's a fucking toe ragged shit.

Cathy I know. I've decided I'm going to punish him.

I came up with a brilliant idea. I can't tell you what it is because it'd really surprise you and you'd probably try and stop me or you'd tell the police and then things would just go from bad to worse.

Isaac Cathy why would I tell the police?

Cathy You wouldn't really. But I bet you'd try and stop me and I've got this smashing idea and it'd really annoy him and don't you think he deserves to be annoyed? (p. 62)

Other images from Euripides' tragedy resonate throughout *Blindsided*. Medea's false gifts to Jason's new bride of a 'finely woven dress' and 'golden diadem', which poison the skin and set alight the hair of the young princess, is echoed in Cathy's present to Siobhan Hennessey; it is only when Siobhan is wearing the dress that Cathy confronts her: 'I should set you on fire or something shouldn't I?' (p. 71). The degree to which geography plays a significant role in both these plays is striking, as is the profoundly Greek convention of significant encounters taking place outside or on the threshold of houses: John and Cathy first meet '*outside the front of her house*' (p. 3); the confrontation between Susan and John takes place '*outside John Connolly's flat*' (p. 29) and when Harry Connolly tracks down Cathy to the Isle of Man they encounter one another in '*the doorway of Cathy Heyer's house in Peel*' (p. 87).

Further to these intertextual references, however, a close reading of *Medea*, particularly of the arguments that Jason

---

[7] Ibid., p. 2, p. 4.

presents to justify his actions, suggests that the political drama at the heart of this tragedy also manifests in the imaginative metabolism of *Blindsided*. In essence, Jason's defence of his decision is based upon the logic of pragmatism and rationalisation: his marriage to King Creon's daughter is, he claims, an act of expediency effected so that his family 'might live well / And not be short of anything' and his children be brought up 'worthily / Of my position'.[8] Medea's role in this exercise is to go into exile; a deal Jason attempts to sweeten:

If you wish [. . .]
In exile to have some of my money to help you,
Say so, for I am prepared to give with an open hand,
Or to provide you with introductions to my friends
Who will treat you well. You are a fool if you do not
Accept this. Cease your anger and you will profit.[9]

In Euripides' *Medea*, Jason is, at base, a businessman; an entrepreneur smoothing the way for the greater acquisition of material goods and worldly reputation. In entering this new 'royal alliance', Jason traduces the bonds of love, commitment, trust and faith that bound him in marriage to Medea. Branding her a 'fool' for 'refus[ing] what is good for you',[10] Jason simultaneously asserts his principles and scorns her reaction to the desecration of her ideals as outmoded, unnecessary and irrational. If we read the political tragedy of *Medea* as the triumph of rationality and instrumentalism over values such as trust, compassion and empathy – values which have no place in Jason's imagined career – then we can begin to trace the play's influence upon *Blindsided*'s political consciousness.

Bracketed by the anticipation of two significant elections – the victory of the Conservative Party, led by Margaret Thatcher, in May 1979 and, seventeen years later, its defeat

---

8 Ibid., p. 18.
9 Ibid., p. 20.
10 Ibid., p. 19, p. 20.

by Tony Blair's New Labour in May 1997 – *Blindsided* is, by his own admission, Stephens's 'most party-political play' to date. Set during the final months of the 'Winter of Discontent' (1978/79), during which the UK experienced widespread public-sector strikes in protest against spending cuts and real-term reductions in wages, the play not only anticipates Thatcher's election to power but is steeped in a horror of, and anger against, the consequent deracination of social, cultural and generational bonds, as well as the insidious erosion of oppositional politics, effected by the social and economic policies of her government. It is no coincidence that it is the morally insecure characters of Cathy and John who register the impact of the strikes, reading them not as instances of political ferment and class solidarity but rather as omens for better things to come under Thatcher:

> **John**   [. . .] Do you ever get the sense that something amazing is going to happen?
>
> The gravediggers have gone on strike. It's completely astonishing. They've stopped burying corpses. It's getting worse so that it can get much, much better. She'll win. At the election. Definitely. The Government'll change. Everything will change. It will be extraordinary. (p. 43)

Cathy's essay on 'the causes and consequences of the Paris Commune' (p. 50), a socialist council established in 1871 and violently suppressed by the French government, similarly serves to exemplify a profound lack of sympathy for, or even identity with, the working classes of which Cathy and her friends and family are a part: 'They were asking for it. If people don't live in order and sense then all you get is chaos. That was my main argument' (ibid.). Significantly, the only character to voice any ambivalence or opposition towards Thatcher is a Jewish refugee from Germany, who fled when his country also democratically elected a leader who promised economic and social 'reform':

Cathy   [. . .] Did you hear? He was right all along wasn't he? Margaret Thatcher was the winner.

Do you think everything's going to change now?

Isaac   Probably. Yeah. It probably will.

Cathy   A new start.

Isaac   Maybe. (p. 85)

The central image of the play – of a child suffocated by its mother while it sleeps – resonates associatively with what Stephens describes as Thatcher's 'murderous' embrace of neoliberal economic doctrine. In her eleven years in power, Thatcher launched a sustained assault on the fabric of British society, curbing trade-union power, withdrawing the commitments of the welfare state, privatising state-owned industry and promoting the creation and acquisition of material wealth (couched in the instrumentalist rationality espoused by Medea's entrepreneurial Jason) as 'an ethic in itself, capable of acting as a guide to all human action, and substituting for all previously held ethical beliefs' and responsibilities.[11] These attacks on the 'social bases of collective action and ideas' worked to erode those 'institutional forms that could make building any alternative [society] possible or even imaginable'[12] and a profound ideological reorientation was effected, in which previously lauded ideals such as community, solidarity and collective action were marginalised and ridiculed, while traits such as individualism, selfishness and greed were celebrated and rewarded.

---

[11] Paul Treanor qtd. David Harvey, *A Brief History of Neoliberalism* (Oxford: Oxford University Press, 2005), p. 3.
[12] Tom Miller, 'The Death of a Class Warrior: Margaret Thatcher 1925–2013', New Left Project, 8 April 2013, www.newleftproject.org/index.php/site/article_comments/the_death_of_a_class_warrior_margaret_thatcher_1925_2013 (accessed 23 December 2013).

Cathy Everything's gone backwards. This whole country's gone upside down. The good things are bad things the bad things are good things. (p. 75).

It is with some poignancy that Part Two of *Blindsided* takes place in the weeks leading up to a second keenly anticipated election. Significantly, these final two scenes present a new departure in Stephens's dramaturgy: while this is his third play to date to follow a protagonist over a period of years (see *Port* and *Country Music*, 2004) it is the first in which, as the stage directions inform us, the protagonist is played by two different actors: 'The same actor who plays Susan Heyer in Part One should play Cathy Heyer in Part Two' (p. 2). Stephens's writing often exposes its artifice through an acknowledgement of the audience's central role in imagining and engaging with the dramatic fiction onstage; here, the formal experimentation is pressed into the service of the play's final, albeit ambivalent, note of optimism.

In the most literal terms possible, the Cathy we meet in Part Two has 'changed': an observation which may seem banal until we remember her previous difficulty in imagining a present or a future in which such a thing were possible:

Cathy [. . .] I thought to myself yesterday, I thought, that no matter what happens now. I'll always be who I am. And the only thing I can change is the things I do. I so wish I could actually turn into somebody completely different. That would be my wildest dream. (p. 43)

'Look at you' she says to Ruthy as she holds up her pillow. 'Imagine growing up as you?' (p. 77). In Part Two, however, Cathy is literally transformed by the realisation that change and renewal form an inevitable, necessary, part of individual – and, by extension, collective – experience:

Cathy [. . .] I changed.

The first day they took me to Staffordshire I sat on a concrete slab and they hosed me down to get rid of all

the nits and the infection and it was exactly at that
moment then that I changed. My whole body changed.
I became a different person with a different body. It was
the saddest feeling ever but in the end it was all okay.
It's a shame it didn't happen earlier. If I'd been a
different person I wouldn't have done the things that I
did. (p.100)

As an audience member witnessing the actor playing
Susan Heyer 'become' Cathy Heyer, we see 'character'
uncoupling from 'actor' and perhaps glimpse, in that
moment of performance, a reminder that individuals cannot
be defined by a single act; that identity is fluid, mutable, *not*
for ever fixed in a determined place and time. The casting of
the actor playing Susan Heyer in the role of her daughter is,
moreover, symmetrically matched in performance by the
casting of the actor playing John Connolly as Harry
Connolly, his son. In its closing moments the play seems to
contemplate the change of not only individuals but also
generations: what it meant to be seventeen or thirty-seven in
1979 was a very different prospect from being seventeen or
thirty-seven in 1997 and now, in 2014, it is different again.
Watching the onstage figures of Susan/Cathy and John/
Harry encounter one another across the generations, united
by the gestures of lifting a face to the rain, and a hand to the
cheek, *Blindsided* concludes with a quiet, sad, hope for
forgiveness and renewal.

Jacqueline Bolton is Lecturer in Drama and Theatre at the
University of Lincoln

Blindsided

Characters

Cathy Heyer
John Connolly
Isaac Berg
Susan Heyer
Siobhan Hennessey
Harry Connolly

Part One is set in Reddish, Stockport in early spring 1979.

Part Two is set in Peel on the Isle of Man in early spring 1997.

An interval might fall more happily between Scenes Eight and Nine than between Parts One and Two.

The same actor who plays John Connolly should play Harry Connolly.

The same actor who plays Susan Heyer in Part One should play Cathy Heyer in Part Two.

Part One

Scene One

John Connolly *and* **Cathy Heyer**. *Outside the front of her house.*

Cathy   What are you doing?

What are you doing outside our house? Are you completely deaf or something?

John   No.

Cathy   Why are you standing outside our house?

John   I'm delivering pamphlets.

Cathy   You're doing what?

John   For the Conservative Party. Have you thought about who you're going to vote for in the next election?

Cathy   Are you being serious?

John   Don't I look it?

Cathy   You don't exactly look like a politician.

John   I'm not a politician.

Cathy   You're not exactly dressed like a politician.

John   I'm not a politician. Can we count on your vote in the next election?

Cathy   You look more like a psychopath than a politician.

John   Flipping heck. I'm not a psychopath either.

Cathy   You look like a serial killer. You look really strange.

John   Thank you.

Cathy   You don't talk like a politician either. A politician wouldn't say 'Flipping heck'. Not right to somebody's face. Why are you dressed like that?

John   Like what?

Cathy   Like that. With your big coat?

John   It's cold.

Cathy   But you're not dressed like somebody dressed for the cold you're dressed like somebody trying to look interesting. Is it cause you're an intellectual?

John   No. What?

Cathy   Is it because you're all sad and gloomy?

John   Can we count on your vote in the next general election?

Cathy   Aren't you a bit young to be in the Conservative Party?

John   Not anymore. Not nowadays. All sorts of people are in the Conservative Party nowadays.

Cathy   Yeah. Mad people.

John   I'm probably going to go now.

Cathy   I should know and all.

John   What do you mean?

Cathy   You're John Connolly.

Pause.

Cathy   You're John Connolly aren't you?

John   How do you know my name?

Cathy   How do you think?

John   I've absolutely no idea.

Cathy   I've watched you every day for the past three weeks.

You live on Southcliffe Road off Reddish Road by the Golf Club. You only just came here. You're training to be an accountant. You're working for Jason Kirkby as his assistant.

You come from Bradwell. In the Hope Valley. Which is a dump. Believe me, if anybody knows whether or not you look sad and gloomy it's me and you do so there you are. You better just live with it because it's actually the truth. I'm Cathy.

Hi.

John   Why were you watching me?

Cathy   I'm interested in new arrivals. Round here you need people to shake things up a bit.

Are you really delivering political pamphlets?

John   Yes.

Cathy   Are you?

John   No.

Cathy   What were you doing here?

John   I was sizing up your house to see the best ways to get in, in order to do a bit of burgling when you weren't around.

Cathy   Were you?

John   Is your Mum in?

Cathy   No.

John   That's good then. Is she normally in at this time of day?

Cathy   Do you honestly think I'm going to answer that question?

John   Are you normally in at this time of day?

Cathy   Not normally.

John   Where are you normally?

Cathy   At college.

John   Stockport College?

Cathy I like your tactics.

John What are you studying at Stockport College?

Cathy A levels.

John Right.

She sucks her thumb.

Cathy That was a lie by the way. I'm not doing A levels. I'm doing one. An A level.

John That's unusual.

Cathy I'm doing an A level in History. It's all I ever think about.

John Why are you sucking your thumb?

Cathy I'm not.

John You are.

Cathy It's funny isn't it?

John What is?

Cathy Are you thinking all kinds of things about me?

John No.

Cathy Are you secretly hoping we're going to spend a certain amount of time together?

John Not in any way.

Cathy If you're going to spend any time at all with me you need to know that I do have a daughter.

John Who said I wanted to spend any time at all with you?

Cathy She's six months old. She's called Ruth. I call her Ruthy. I love her completely. She smells like the most beautiful thing that was ever on earth. She can't sleep properly and sometimes that tires me out I have to confess. I don't know who her dad is. It could be one of several men. I never bothered trying to find out. Quite quickly after I got pregnant with her I realised they were pretty much redundant. Fathers.

John Are you trying to impress me, or something?

Cathy Not in any way. It's just something I genuinely believe. My own dad died when I was twelve, for example, and I can honestly say I don't think I'm in any way worse off for the experience.

John Are you asking me to feel sorry for you?

Cathy He was a hairdresser.

He isn't altogether certain how to respond to this. She doesn't leave him much time.

Do you like the way I smell?

John I've not really noticed it.

Cathy Do you know what smell that is?

John No.

Cathy It's Oil of Ulay.

John Terrific.

Cathy When I'm not in college I work at the butcher's on Manchester Road and sometimes I do smell a bit of meat so I take particular care to have a good wash as soon as I possibly can and I find Oil of Ulay the best means of washing the smell off.

John It smells lovely.

Cathy Thank you very much. Do you like being a junior accountant? Don't answer that. I don't really want to know. I'll tell you something for nothing John Connolly. I'm not surprised people go on strikes.

You get to have a day off work. If *I* was a bin man around here I'd go on strike. Definitely. People drop so much litter around here they should be ashamed of themselves.

John   Do you ever stop talking?

Cathy   Not when I'm nervous.

John   I'd very much like to meet her.

Cathy   Who?

John   Your daughter.

Pause.

Cathy   You wouldn't.

John   I would.

It starts to rain.

Cathy   It's raining.

John   Yeah.

Cathy   Do this.

John   What?

Cathy   Lift your face up. It's lovely isn't it?

She lifts her face up to the rain. He watches her. He does it too. He looks at her.

John   Have you got a boyfriend?

Cathy   No. Have you?

John   Of course not.

Cathy   Have you got a girlfriend then?

John   No I haven't.

Cathy   That's a relief.

John   Why?

Cathy   Why do you flipping think? You're not married are you?

John   No.

Cathy   Neither am I. I wish I was. Sometimes I feel like I am. In my mind I'm married to Evel Knievel.

John   Gosh.

Cathy   Only when I'm kind of playing.

Do you want to go for a walk?

John   Where do you want to walk to?

Cathy   I don't really care I just quite like the idea of walking down a road chatting to you.

Were you really scouting our house to try to break into it?

John   Yes. I was. I'm sorry.

Cathy   Have you ever really broken into somebody's house?

John   Yes.

Cathy   Have you?

John   Yes.

Cathy   I think you're completely lying.

John   I don't rob poor people's houses and I never take anything that might be of the remotest sentimental value. But I really do break into other people's houses when I'm bored. I've never hurt anybody. I would, of course, if I felt it was the only means of self-defence.

Cathy   What's it like?

Scene Two

Cathy and **John**. *Inside* **Isaac**'s *house. Three days later.*

As they talk he kisses her.

Cathy   You're a bit mental aren't you?

John   No.

Cathy   You are. Like a deranged person.

John   Shut up.

Cathy   Like a retard. Like a fucking spastic.

He kisses her ears. He bites her neck.

Cathy   Oh fuck that's lovely.

John   What is?

Cathy   You kissing my ears. It's like an electric shock.

John   Do you ever want to break things?

Cathy   Yeah.

John   What kind of things do you think about breaking?

Cathy   I like throwing bricks through windows. I like setting fire to stuff. I set fire to a park bench once.

She unbuckles his belt. She undoes his trousers. She rubs his cock.

Cathy   I like cutting bits of other people's hair off.

Sometimes I like to do pisses on things.

John   Pisses?

Cathy   I pissed on my gran's carpet in her bathroom on purpose one time.

That was funny cause she thought it was my mate's brother.

John   Well she would.

Cathy   I know.

John   Girls don't piss on the floor by accident. Boys do all the time.

Cathy   That was kind of why I did it.

She takes his cock out of his pants. She goes down on him.

John   Oh Christ.

Cathy   What?

John   Nothing. Don't stop.

Cathy   You're funny.

John   Please.

She stops before he comes. She stands up. She takes her knickers off from beneath her dress and puts them in his pocket. She examines his face.

Cathy   I like your left ear.

John   What?

Cathy   Is that a bit random?

Your right one's okay. Your left one's flipping brilliant.

She smiles.

You're quite scared aren't you?

John   Not in any way.

Cathy   You are. Don't worry. I like it. Bite me.

John   What?

Cathy   Bite my cheek.

He does. She puts him inside her. They fuck. She comes.

She hits him repeatedly for making her come. Some time.

Cathy   Your skin is just about the most incredible skin in the world has anybody ever said that to you before?

John   No.

Cathy   Well they really should have done because it's true. I could wrap myself up in your skin and sleep there all night. You have a lovely, lovely cock too, which is nice.

John   Right. Thank you.

Cathy   That's okay.

They lie there for some time.

Cathy   Are you okay? John?

John   Ssshhh.

Cathy   Ha.

John   Why are you laughing?

Cathy   No reason. I wasn't. I like it.

John   What?

Cathy   Lying here.

They lie for some time.

I love this feeling.

They lie there for some time.

I feel like every bit of me is awake and asleep at the same time.

They lie there for some time.

If I tell you something do you promise not to have an epileptic fit?

John   It depends what it is.

Cathy   You need to promise.

John   I can't do that you're going to have to try me out.

Cathy   When I'm with you. I don't worry about all the things that have happened to me. And I don't worry about the things that are going to happen. I don't worry about Ruthy. I feel like I'm kind of just there.

John   I've known you three days Cathy.

Cathy   I can get rather attached to people quite suddenly.

It's funny this.

John   Why?

Cathy   Breaking into somebody else's house.

John   Do you think he'll notice we've been here?

Cathy   I don't know. I'll make the bed before we go. Have a bit of a tidy up.

John   Don't.

Cathy   I've never seen his bed before.

John   Haven't you?

Cathy   No. Why would I? I always wanted to be a criminal.

John   And now you are.

Cathy   Does it count if you know the person whose house it is, really well?

John   Of course it counts. He didn't let you in here, did he?

Cathy   No he definitely didn't.

John   What does he do?

Cathy   He's a hairdresser too. He went to school with my dad. And then he became his apprentice. When my dad died he really looked after my mum.

John   Was he trying to get in her pants?

Cathy   He's very attentive to her. He's been very good with Ruthy. He babysits sometimes. If I'm not careful I'll start feeling a bit guilty.

John   What would he do if he came back and found us?

Cathy   He'd be a bit surprised.

John   How will you tell him we got in?

Cathy   I'll tell him my mum gave me a key.

John   You should change your hair.

Cathy   Why?

John   You should wear it up or something. Or wear it down. I don't know. Change the colour.

Cathy   Why?

John   It would look better.

Some time.

Cathy   I don't know anything about you.

John   No. It's good isn't it?

Cathy   Ssshhh.

John   What?

Cathy   Did you hear something?

John   No.

Cathy   I heard something.

John   You didn't.

Cathy   I did.

John   You definitely didn't.

Isaac Berg *enters.*

Isaac   Hello. Cathy.

Cathy   Hello Isaac.

Isaac   This is a bit of a surprise.

Cathy   Yes. I'm sure it must be. I can explain.

Isaac   Right.

Cathy   I can't really.

Isaac   No.

Cathy   This is John.

Isaac   Hello.

John   Hello Isaac. I've heard absolutely everything about you.

Isaac   Have you?

John   Absolutely everything. All about Cathy's dad and the hairdressing business in general and how attentive you've been to Cathy's mum and your level of concern for little baby Ruthy. Cathy's done an excellent job of building you up before your arrival so I have to say it's really quite exciting to meet you.

Cathy   John's my boyfriend.

Isaac   I see.

John   She's known me three days.

Isaac   How did you get in here?

John   I mean I kind of am her boyfriend but I've never heard her use that word before and I have only known her for three days so I'm slightly taken aback by her tone of familiarity.

Cathy   Mum gave me a key. We didn't expect you to be back. We just needed somewhere to go and I asked Mum if it would be all right if we came round here and she said it would be so we did.

Isaac   When you say you needed somewhere to go?

Cathy   We don't really get a great deal of opportunity to be alone with each other.

Isaac   I don't know how I feel about that.

Cathy   No. I'm sorry Isaac.

John   It's not true by the way.

Cathy   What?

John   She didn't borrow her mum's key. We broke in. Your bathroom window was really easy to prise open. It's just something I sometimes do. Break into people's houses. It's smashing fun. Can I say, in the face of what must be rather surprising news you're being terrifically calm and I admire that immensely. We didn't damage anything. They'll be minor superficial damage to the window frame but it's not much more than a few chips of paint.

Isaac I should call the police.

John Don't be ridiculous.

Isaac How is that ridiculous? I come home. I have absolutely no idea who you are. Cathy's here. She's in my bed. You've clearly been. You've been.

John We did have a bit of a fuck. It was a really good one. It was releasing.

Isaac I'm going to call your mum and then I'm going to call the police.

Cathy Isaac. Don't.

John He won't.

Isaac Watch me.

John If you do I promise you I'll find you and I'll beat the living shit out of you.

Cathy John.

John I have got one fuck of a temper on me haven't I Cathy?

Cathy He really has.

John So just calm down.

Cathy His dad was a farmer. He inherits it from him.

John *wanders off. As he passes* **Isaac**, **Isaac** *backs away.*

John See?

Isaac *looks at him.*

John You flinched. He flinched.

He winks at them and exits. **Cathy** *and* **Isaac** *left alone.*

Cathy Isaac I'm really sorry he threatened to beat the living shit out of you.

Isaac   Who is he?

Cathy   He's called John Connolly. He's a trainee accountant. Would you like me to clean your sheets? I could put some spare ones on your bed. It's nice. Isn't it? The feeling of clean sheets on a bed. Don't look like that.

Isaac   Like what?

Cathy   You look really worried. You look really strange.

Scene Three

John *and* **Cathy** *and* **Susan Heyer**, **Cathy***'s mother. The Heyer front room. Afternoon.*

John   Cathy's always going on about you.

She's fond of you. Some people really take to their mothers don't they? She takes to you. She looks a bit like you as well I think. You've both startling eyes. I brought you this.

He presents her with the gift of a toasty maker.

Susan   What is it?

John   It's a toastie machine. It makes toasties. It's like a toaster but you open it from the top and it toasts sandwiches on both the bottom and the top half and kind of presses them together. I'm sorry that it's not in a box and I think it is actually second hand but I thought you might find it useful.

I like your hair.

Susan   You what?

John   Sorry is that a bit much. I always misjudge these things don't I?

Cathy   You do sometimes.

John   She'll tell you. 'John,' she says. 'You always misjudge these things. You're always a bit much.'

Susan   How long have you been going out with my daughter?

John   Twelve days.

Susan   Isaac told me he found you in his house.

John   Did he?

Cathy   I'm really sorry Mum.

Susan   You should be ashamed of yourselves.

Cathy   Would you like a cup of coffee John?

John   Yes. Please. That would be terrific. Me and coffee. I'm coffee bonkers. Aren't I Cathy?

Cathy   He is, yeah. Would you like a cup Mum?

Susan   No. I wouldn't. No.

Cathy   I'll be right back.

She leaves.

John   Can I assure you Mrs Heyer that my intentions towards your daughter are entirely honourable?

Susan   What?

John   I am going to really look after her and really take care of her and as long as she will allow me to I swear I am not going to let her go hungry or get very chilly or be frightened. Nobody will ever batter her. She won't ever need to work but she can if she wants to. I just am going to make her life completely brilliant.

Susan   Shut up.

John   OK.

Susan   Stop gibbering on, for goodness sake.

John   He told me he wouldn't tell.

Susan   Well he did.

John   Where's Ruthy?

Susan   She's asleep. Where do you think she is? She was awake all night.

John   Do you not mind when Cathy stays over at mine?

Susan   Why should I mind?

John   Does it not bother you having to look after Ruthy on your own?

Susan   She's easy to look after. Compared to Cathy she's no trouble at all.

John   Don't say that.

Susan   What?

John   Don't be mean about Cathy. The way she talks about you.

You should get double locks on your windows by the way.

Susan   Why?

John   They're weak. Or get a burglar alarm. Even if it's just the box for a burglar alarm. Put it on the wall outside your house. That'd do the trick as well as anything.

Cathy *comes in with* **John**'s *coffee.*

Cathy   Here.

John   Thank you.

Cathy   You two been chatting about me behind my back, I bet.

Susan   We haven't.

John   We have actually. Does she lie a lot your mum?

Cathy   No. Don't be silly.

Susan   He's a bit superior isn't he?

Cathy   Who?

Susan   Your boyfriend.

Cathy   Mum.

John   Ha.

Cathy   He 's just standing right there.

Susan   Is it true you're a junior accountant?

John   That's right.

Cathy   He works for Jason Kirkby.

Susan   You're not from round here are you?

Cathy   He's from Bradwell. In Derbyshire.

Susan   I've never been there.

John   It's in a place called the Hope Valley. It's beautiful. It's built on limestone. I like the idea that the whole town is built up on coral reefs and marine life that rose up from the sea millions and millions of years ago.

Susan   I don't really know what to say about that.

John   No.

He walks out.

Susan   Where's he gone?

Cathy   I don't know.

Susan   He can't just walk out like that can he?

Cathy   Maybe he's going to the bathroom or something.

Susan   He's really odd. He's really unpleasant. I don't like him one bit.

Cathy   Don't say that.

Susan   You could do a lot better.

Cathy   Mum.

Susan   Are you making our tea or am I?

Cathy   I can.

Susan   Is he stopping?

Cathy   I don't know.

Susan   Does he eat tea?

Cathy   Course he does.

Susan   He's not one of those weirdo types who never eats, is he?

Cathy   How was Ruthy?

Susan   She slept like an angel.

Cathy   Thank you for looking after her.

Susan   Well she's practically my own in a way isn't she?

Cathy   She likes it when you're there.

Susan   I changed her four times. Twice in the middle of the night. She smelt a bit funny. Her number twos.

Cathy   John asked me to move in with him.

I told him I would.

I'm going to move in next week. I'm going to take Ruthy with me.

Susan *looks at her for some time*.

Cathy   I don't expect you to say anything. I just thought it was fair to let you know.

Susan   Are you joking?

Cathy   No.

Susan   You do realise that there is absolutely no way I am going to let you leave.

Cathy   What do you mean 'let me leave'?

Susan   And if you do you're not taking Ruthy.

Cathy   I am.

Pause.

I love him Mum.

Susan   You don't know what love is.

Cathy   I've never felt anything like it.

Susan   He puts his hand in your knickers and promises you the world. It's nothing.

Cathy   Well if this is nothing I don't know what something is.

I watch him sleeping. He never snores. He looks like a baby. Can I tell you one thing I do? Sometimes when he's not in I put his clothes on.

John *returns.*

John   I hope you don't mind me walking out on you like that. I just found myself getting unnecessarily irritated and I thought that the best thing to do was to extract myself from the situation. You have a beautiful house Mrs Heyer. You must be proud. I wanted to see Ruthy. I've never seen her before. She's fast asleep. She looks quite peaceful when she's asleep doesn't she? Are her limbs meant to be at those angles? Funny isn't it? The feelings we have for our children. I have to say the extent to which your eyes look exactly like Cathy's is overwhelming me a touch. Do you mind if I don't stay for my tea. I should be getting back. Maybe both us should, Cathy. Sometimes you know when you're just not wanted, don't you?

Scene Four

On a picnic blanket in Reddish Vale, **Siobhan Hennessey** *and* **John** *and* **Cathy***. They're drinking cider.*

Cathy *lies on* **John***'s lap.* **Siobhan** *sings 'Hush Little Baby' to Ruthy.*

Cathy *has had her hair cut a lot shorter.*

Cathy   She likes that.

Siobhan   It's cause she can hear my heart beat.

Cathy   It's not. It's because she likes people singing to her. She likes you singing to her especially. You've got a beautiful voice. Hasn't she John?

John   It's all right.

Cathy   Have you heard him? 'It's all right'. You sing like an angel.

Siobhan   She's funny isn't she?

Cathy   How?

Siobhan   With her little movements. I've not seen them before. And her little eyes. Her eyes are so pretty.

Some time.

John   It's warm.

Siobhan   Yeah.

Some time.

Siobhan   When did you get your hair cut, Cathy?

Cathy   Last week.

Siobhan   It looks very different.

Cathy   It's meant to. Do you like it?

Siobhan   I love it. It shows your eyes up.

Cathy   I got it done how John asked me to have it done.

Siobhan   Did you?

Cathy   Is there something wrong with that?

Siobhan   Not really.

Some time.

Should I cut my hair too do you think?

Cathy   That's up to you.

Siobhan   Should I cut it as short as you?

Cathy   No.

Siobhan   What do you think?

Cathy   What's it got to do with him?

Siobhan   What do you think John?

John   No. You should leave it exactly like that.

Some time.

Cathy   It's lovely here.

Siobhan   Yeah.

Some time.

John   It stinks a bit now, though, doesn't it? People are so bloody lazy. They should take their rubbish away themselves. One day, soon, everybody's going to go on strike.

Cathy   You'd love that. Look at his face. The way he talks about it.

Siobhan   I like it.

Cathy   What?

Siobhan   His face.

Cathy   Shiv.

Siobhan   Sorry.

Cathy   That's not really exactly appropriate.

Siobhan   It is true though. Do you know who you look like?

John   Who?

Siobhan   John Travolta.

Cathy   You should see him in his underpants. It's less exciting then, I'll tell you that for nothing.

Siobhan   I can imagine.

Cathy   He doesn't even know how to pair his socks. He never bloody washes a plate.

Siobhan   Is she always like this to you?

John   Pretty much.

Cathy   I am not.

Siobhan   Is it really lovely living together?

John   It is yes.

Siobhan   Do you have all kind of little routines as well?

Cathy   Yes.

John   We don't. Don't listen to her. We don't.

Cathy   I get home from college or work. He watches the telly. I give him a beer. He watches the telly. I make his tea. He watches telly. I sort Ruthy out. He watches telly. I pour him a bath. He gets in it.

John   She sucks my cock.

Pause.

Well, you do.

Siobhan   Do you?

Cathy *can't speak.*

John   She does. She's really good at it.

Siobhan   Are you?

Cathy   I wish I had time frankly. I'm putting Ruthy to bed. I'm doing my homework. I'm trying to wash the stink of the butcher's out of me.

Some time.

John   I like Saturdays.

Some time.

Have we got any more cider?

Siobhan   No.

Cathy   Would you like me to go and get some? What are you grinning about?

Siobhan   I've just missed you. It's really nice to see you. It's really nice to meet you John.

John   Yes. It's absolutely enchanting to meet you too. Does anybody want to go for a walk?

Cathy   No thank you.

John   We could explore.

Siobhan   There's not much to explore I can tell you.

John   I bet I could find somewhere.

I can always find something to explore, me. Always find somewhere to go. Something to do. Someone to play with. We wouldn't have to bring little Spazzy Bones with us would we? Sorry. That's just an affectionate little nickname I just made up for her just now this second. Was it really horrible? You know I don't mean it. I've rather taken to her. I have, Cathy. Do you forgive me? Cathy, please will you forgive me for calling Ruthy 'spazzy bones' and suggesting we leave her here in the middle of the Vale?

Cathy *examines* **John**.

Cathy   Why are you looking at her like that?

John   Like what?

Cathy   Don't say like what it just makes it worse.

John   I honestly don't know what you're going on about.

Cathy   I don't blame him Shiv you're beautiful. He's eating you up with his eyes.

She takes Ruthy and puts her in her buggy and prepares to leave.

Siobhan   Where are you going?

Cathy   I'm going getting more cider. I said.

John   Good thinking.

Cathy   Do you want to come with me John?

John   I'm a bit knackered. I just want to have a bit of a kip.

Cathy   Please.

John   No.

Siobhan   It's all right. He can stay here. I'll make sure nobody robs him in his sleep.

Cathy   I will be back.

She leaves pushing Ruthy in her buggy.

Siobhan   If you want to have a sleep I'll watch your bag and everything. I promise not to run off.

John   I don't. I'm not tired in the least. I was just feeling a bit bored.

Siobhan   Yeah.

John   Cathy tells me you've got your own flat.

Siobhan   It's council. Northumberland Parade. On Northumberland Road. Flat 5c.

John   Lovely. And you work at Boots.

Siobhan   On Merseyway.

John   Is that thrilling?

Siobhan   No.

John   Don't you just love being surrounded by chemicals?

Siobhan   Some chemicals are quite fun.

John   Do you think you'll stay working in Boots for years and years Siobhan?

Siobhan   No.

John   What else do you want to do?

Siobhan   I don't really know.

John   Do you want to stay in Stockport?

Siobhan   May as well.

John   You like it do you?

Siobhan   I do, yeah.

John   What do you like about it?

She looks at him. Doesn't know what to say.

I see.

Siobhan   Are you really going to beat Isaac up?

John   No.

Siobhan   You should. He's a soft bastard.

John   It's not that he's soft. He's not soft at all. It's that he thinks he's wise. He's not.

Siobhan   I would have loved to see his face when you threatened him.

She makes a sudden movement to him. He flinches.

'You flinched. He flinched.'

John   I like your arms

Siobhan   You what?

John   It's nice, looking at your arms.

They look at each other.

Siobhan   Have you ever done this?

John   What?

Siobhan   This.

She rubs her arm against his.

John   Its nice isn't it?

Siobhan   And what about this?

She tickles the underside of his arm.

John   That tickles.

Siobhan   Yeah.

John   Are you ticklish?

Siobhan   I am a bit.

John   I thought you would be.

Where are you most ticklish?

Siobhan   On my tummy.

John   Show me.

Siobhan   What?

John   Show me your tummy.

Cathy *comes back in.*

Cathy   Were you talking about, me?

Siobhan   No.

Cathy   I bet you were. People do. Constantly jibber
jabbering. They think they're doing it behind my back.
They're not. I can always hear them. I completely can hear
you by the way.

Scene Five

Outside **John***'s flat.* **John** *and* **Susan**.

John   Mrs Heyer, what a delightful surprise.

Susan   Is Cathy in?

John   No.

Susan   Good.

John   Why's that good?

Susan   I wanted to speak to you on your own.

John   How exciting.

Susan   Why aren't you at work?

John   I slept in.

Susan   It's gone eleven o'clock.

John   I know. It's slightly shameful. Me and Cathy were, well we were up rather late I'm afraid to admit. We didn't get a great deal of sleep last night, either of us.

Susan   I don't want to know.

John   I bet you do. Sorry it's Cathy and I isn't it? I'm always making that mistake. I called Mr Kirkby. He was initially livid but I talked him down. I was on my way out just now as a matter of fact.

Susan   Where is she now?

John   At college.

Susan   Where's Ruthy?

John   She's gone with her. They've got a play school.

Susan   You're not looking after her?

John   No.

Susan   Well that's a relief. I wouldn't trust you with her for all the tea in the world.

Pause.

John   Are you sure you meant that?

Susan   What?

John   I mean ordinarily it's all the tea in China. Or all the money in the world. I've never heard anybody get those two things mixed up before. I mean fair play. There's plenty

more tea in the world than just in China. Tea all over India
for example.

Susan   Stop talking.

John   There's a small amount of tea in here. Would you
like one?

Susan   No I wouldn't no.

John   Will you come in?

Susan   No.

John   Come in.

Susan   No.

John   We can't stand out here talking everybody'll stare.
Who knows what they'll think? Is that a new top?

Susan   I beg your pardon?

John   Your top. Is it new? It's rather fetching. I like it. It
suits you.

Susan   Shut your mouth John Connolly.

John   I'm sorry. Was I being rude? I thought I was offering
you a compliment.

Susan   I can tell, you know.

John   You can tell what?

Susan   Don't think I can't because I can. I'm not a
complete idiot.

John   Aren't you?

Susan   Have you got someone in there now? Is she hiding
under your bed?

Some time. He looks at her.

John   Are you mad?

Susan   Should I come in and have a look.

John   I keep asking you to.

Susan   I know you John Connolly. I've known men like you for years and years. I think it would be better for everybody if you just left the whole place well alone.

He looks at her. Smiles.

John   Funny isn't it? You could be sisters, you and Cathy couldn't you? I mean sisters with an unusual age gap but sisters nevertheless. Does anybody ever make that mistake? Do you ever pop down the pub and the landlord asks you what your sister's having to drink? You've got to watch those landlords haven't you? They can be right rum buggers. Little dirty minded shits.

Susan   Don't you dare lie to my little girl.

John   I'm not lying. I don't lie.

Susan   Don't you dare think you're taking her away from me because you're really not going to do that.

John   Does she belong to you?

Let me tell you something for nothing Suzy Q, if you come round to my flat talking to me like that one more time I swear I will flatten you.

Susan   You don't frighten me. You're a little boy.

John   That girl would do anything I told her to.

Susan   She fucking wouldn't.

John   You want to try me?

Pause.

Can I ask you something, Susan, how old were you when the old man died?

She doesn't respond.

What was his name?

She doesn't respond.

Susan, I'm sorry for teasing you. I'm being a right little cheeky chops and I know it's unfair because let's be honest with each other here, you're hardly the sharpest knife in the drawer are you? I think the two of us must have got off on the wrong foot. We're practically family for goodness sake! Just tell me what his name was. Cathy hasn't told me. She never talks about him. I think she really misses him by the way although she'd tell you the opposite. Sometimes we do that don't we? Say the absolute polar opposite to what we actually mean. What was his name?

Susan   Edward.

John   Did you used to call him that or did you used to call him Ed? Or Eddy, perhaps?

Susan   I used to call him Edward.

John   And how old were you when he died?

Susan   That's none of your business.

John   No. I know. I'm just nosey. How old were you?

Susan   Thirty-two.

John   Ripe.

Pause.

Susan   Why did you come here?

John   It's my flat.

Susan   To Stockport. Why did you leave Bradwell?

John   I outgrew the place.

Susan   Why did you end up here?

John   It was a bit random I have to admit. I just fancied a change. It's the kind of thing I do. I might move again, you know? Take Cathy with me. Pop Ruthy in the car seat. Head off into the sunset.

Susan   You wouldn't.

John   Wouldn't I?

Susan   She wouldn't go with you. She'd never take Ruthy. She'd never do that.

Scene Six

Siobhan's *flat.* **Siobhan** *and* **John**.

John   It's a smashing view.

Siobhan   Yeah.

John   You can see the Pennines.

Do you ever go there?

Siobhan   No.

John   You should you know? I miss it, the countryside.

Siobhan   We went with school. We went on a school camping trip to Edale.

I was twelve. It was brilliant. It was sunny all week. We walked to the top of Kinder Scout. I'm sorry. I'm talking a lot. I'm a bit nervous.

John   What are you nervous for?

Siobhan   I'm not used to having visitors.

John   No?

Siobhan   No.

John   It might be your nervousness that puts them off.

Siobhan   It might be.

John   Or your talking.

Siobhan   Do you want a cup of tea?

John   No thank you.

Siobhan   Don't you like tea?

John   Not really, no.

Siobhan   How's Cathy?

John   She's completely fantastic thank you very much for asking. You should come round. Come and see Ruthy. Give us a bit of a song.

She doesn't answer.

How many plug sockets are there in this room?

Siobhan   I don't know. Three. Four, there's one behind the door. Why?

John   No reason.

Are all these windows in all these flats locked from the inside?

He reaches over to her hair and runs his hands through it.

Does that feel nice?

Siobhan   Extremely.

John   Do you know how many nerve endings there are in your scalp?

Siobhan   No.

John   Bloody loads.

Siobhan   I bet.

John   I love it.

Siobhan   What?

He smiles. Pulls his hand away.

John   Your flat.

Siobhan   Thanks.

John   If my mother could see me now.

Siobhan   You what?

John   How's work?

Siobhan   Shit.

John   Why?

Siobhan   It's always shit.

John   Is it?

Siobhan   At the moment it's worse than normal.

John   Why?

Siobhan   Because of the strikes. There's absolutely fucking nothing coming into the shop. We're just left there looking like muppets.

What?

John   You.

Siobhan   What about me?

John   You're surprisingly energetic aren't you?

Siobhan   I don't know.

John   I like it. It's a quality I'm drawn to in Cathy as well. She's not as smart as you but she's got a similar kind of energy.

Siobhan   Cathy's smart.

John   Yeah.

Siobhan   She's like a force of nature.

John   Yeah.

Siobhan   She's my best friend.

He kisses her. She kisses him back.

Siobhan   Don't.

John   Why not?

Siobhan   You know why not. I can't.

John   You can.

Siobhan   Please John. I don't even fancy you that much.

John   Don't you?

Siobhan   I don't fancy you half as much as you fancy yourself.

John   How many times do you think I'd need to stroke your hair like this, with my nails, before you dragged me into your bedroom?

Siobhan   It won't work.

John   Do you think you could stand a hundred?

Siobhan   No.

John   Fifty.

Siobhan   More like five.

She punches his chest quite hard. He smiles at her and backs away a bit.

Siobhan   Sorry.

John   You should be.

Siobhan   Can we just?

John   What?

Siobhan   Not.

John   Okay.

Some time.

Siobhan   How's the apprenticeship going Johnny Connolly?

John   It's terrific.

Siobhan   Why aren't you there today?

John   Mr Kirkby's a bit poorly. He didn't come in. I had some work to do.

I finished it early so that I could come round and see you.

Siobhan   What work?

John   Filing the VAT returns before Friday. Funny isn't it?

Siobhan   What is?

John   You say just that one sentence 'filing the VAT returns before Friday' and it immediately saps all sexual energy in the room. How many people live on each floor here?

Siobhan   I don't know.

John   How many flats are there?

Siobhan   Ten.

John   Nobody would notice would they?

Siobhan   Notice what?

John   If I came back here with Cathy and we broke into one.

Siobhan   I think they would.

John   We can't stop ourselves. We keep trying to. It's just a bit addictive.

Do you mind if I go next door when I've finished here? To scout the place out?

Siobhan   No.

John   Who is it?

Siobhan   It's a guy I think he's a student. I think he's something. I'm not sure.

He plays a lot of Joy Division.

John   Cheery. Does he live on his own?

Siobhan   I think so.

John   Does he have any pets?

Siobhan   No.

John   No dogs or anything like that?

Siobhan   No.

John   Where's your bedroom?

Siobhan   I'm not telling you.

John   I'll find it myself.

Siobhan   Find it yourself then.

John   If you tell anybody that I've been here you know what'll happen don't you?

Siobhan   No.

John   I've got a temper on me the like of which you wouldn't believe.

Siobhan   How's Isaac's face doing? Looked pretty intact when I last saw it.

John   Make us a sandwich will you?

Siobhan   What kind of sandwich?

John   Don't really care. Ham. Chicken. Not cheese. I'll wait for you.

Siobhan   Where?

John   In your room. Don't take ages about it. If you're too long it's not out of the question that I'll end up falling to sleep or something. And we wouldn't want that would we?

Scene Seven

A beach at Blackpool. **John** *and* **Cathy**. *Night is falling.*

Cathy   Are you okay?

John   I'm fine.

Cathy   How's your leg feeling?

John   It's in agony.

Cathy   I'll kiss it better for you.

John   Later.

Cathy   Have you calmed down now?

John   Yeah. Yes. Yes I have. Yes.

Cathy   I hate it when you're like that. Snapping out all over the place.

Blaming everybody for everything.

John   I know.

Cathy   They didn't catch you.

John   No.

Cathy   You didn't take anything anyway did you?

John   No I didn't.

Cathy   They couldn't charge you with anything. You were just standing there.

He doesn't respond.

I wish I'd seen it.

John   It wasn't funny.

Cathy   I bet you looked like Spiderman or something.

John   I didn't.

Cathy   Swinging from a web. Four floors up.

John   It was fucking scary Cathy. It wasn't funny.

Cathy   Did you get a close look up on his face?

John   He was a skinny little shit. I didn't hang around to find out his name or anything like that.

Cathy   You could have battered him probably, knowing you.

John   Yeah.

Cathy   It's like having my own private Alsatian dog. I love it. Poor baby.

I love it here. We used to come here with Dad. Come on Cathy let's go up Blackpool. He'd take us to the funfair. Ruthy likes it here.

John   Does she?

Cathy   Should see her little face.

John   I can imagine.

She looks at him.

We should have brought her with us.

Cathy   Mum was fine. She likes feeling wanted. I didn't tell her what time we'll be back.

She could sleep there, couldn't she?

John   I'd rather go and fetch her.

Cathy   Be better if she stayed though. That way we don't need to wake her.

John   She'll wake up anyway.

Cathy   We could just let Mum deal with it.

John   I'd quite like to pick her up.

She smiles at him.

John   What?

Cathy   You.

John   What about me?

Cathy   You prefer her to me half the time I think. Don't worry. I like it. I'm just a bit surprised.

Some time.

John   We should stop one day you know? Robbing other people's houses.

Cathy   I don't know if I could stop now. It's addictive.

John   If they ever catch me and they find out about my record in Bradwell they'll go mental.

Cathy   They won't catch you. They're not exactly that smart.

I bet that's the real reason you left. Cause the police were on your trail.

He doesn't answer.

I quite like the idea of you being on the run. You're an outlaw. Both of us are when you think about it. I don't know if it's very good for Ruthy to be raised by outlaws. I wonder what my dad would say if he'd seen me. Hi Dad. It's me, Cathy. I'm sitting here on Blackpool beach with a convicted house burglar and being his sidekick.

John   He can't hear you.

Cathy   I know.

Some time.

I wish you'd met him. I miss him like mad sometimes. Sometimes I don't. Do you want to go to the funfair?

John   No.

Cathy   We could go on the pier then.

John   No thank you.

Cathy   Why not? The pier's brilliant here.

John   It's full of old people.

Cathy   Don't be stupid.

John   It is.

Cathy   What's wrong with old people, anyway?

John   I've had enough of them.

Cathy   Why?

John All they do is go on and on and on.

Do you ever get the sense that something amazing is going to happen?

The gravediggers have gone on strike. It's completely astonishing. They've stopped burying corpses. It's getting worse so that it can get much, much better. She'll win. At the election. Definitely. The Government'll change. Everything will change. It will be extraordinary.

Cathy Sshh.

John What?

Cathy Stop talking.

John Why?

Cathy Just listen.

John To what?

Cathy The sea.

They listen to the sea.

Are your mum and dad still alive John?

Don't you want to introduce them to Ruthy?

John She's better off without them, believe me.

Cathy You're almost like her dad now aren't you?

He smiles.

I thought to myself yesterday, I thought, that no matter what happens now. I'll always be who I am. And the only thing I can change is the things I do. I so wish I could actually turn into somebody completely different. That would be my wildest dream. The only time I don't think that is when I'm with you.

You do realise that no matter how hard you look you will never find anybody else who loves you as much as I do don't you?

John   Yes.

Cathy   You couldn't live without me could you?

John   No. I don't think I could.

Cathy   You should marry me is what you should do.

John   Marry you?

Cathy   Yeah. I could be Cathy Connolly. Sometimes I write that down.

Cathy Connolly. Ruth Connolly. Don't you think it sounds nice?

John   It does, yeah.

Cathy   Do you want to?

John   What?

Cathy   Do you want to marry me?

John   Okay.

Cathy   Do you?

John   Yeah. Okay.

Cathy   Will you get me a ring?

John   Do you want one?

Cathy   Yeah. We could get one from one of the machines in the funfair.

Ha! Are we engaged to be married now?

John   I don't know.

Cathy   Am I your fiancée now John?

John   Yeah.

Some time.

Cathy   Don't you think that's funny?

John   What?

Cathy Don't you think that was the best way to get engaged ever? We should mark it.

John Mark it?

Cathy We should have some kind of symbol or something?

John Like what?

Cathy I don't know. You think of something. It's your engagement too you know.

John I can't think.

Cathy Well that's not the first time is it?

John We could have a dance.

Cathy Here?

John Yeah.

Cathy Okay. You nutter. Stand up then. Come on John Connolly. On your feet.

She drags him up.

There's no music.

John No.

Cathy Didn't think of that did you?

John Sorry.

Cathy There's music from the fairground. We've just got to listen a bit harder than you ordinarily would.

They dance together straining hard to listen to the old fifties doo-wop ballad blaring from the fairground. They stop. She leans into him.

Should we have a bit of a fuck?

John In a bit. My leg's still sore.

Cathy You could lie down. You could be Evel Knievel and you've had a horrible motorbike crash. I could be your nurse and I just can't keep my hands off you.

John   That sounds fun.

Cathy   Should we?

He smiles at her.

Some time.

Cathy   We could stay here couldn't we?

John   What?

Cathy   Stay here. Us two. Leave Ruthy with Mum. The pair of them.

She'd love that, Mum.

And never go back?

Do you promise?

Scene Eight

Susan's *house.* **Susan** *and* **Isaac**.

They look at each other. Neither wanting to make the first move.

Isaac   I understand that it's hard.

I've seen you around his sort before.

I've watched her with him myself. She feels like a daughter to me too sometimes. I know that sounds irrational but it's also true.

Susan   It isn't.

Isaac   I've known her all her life.

Susan   That doesn't mean you've got any idea what it's like having a daughter. I'm sorry Isaac, I didn't mean to be rude.

Isaac   You did. It's fine. You're angry.

Susan   I'm not angry, I'm frightened.

He looks at her.

He made a pass at me. He told me he thought I was sexy. Don't tell me you think that's normal because it isn't.

Isaac   I don't really believe in normal behaviour Susan.

Susan   You wouldn't.

Isaac   I think normality in this country is something that's invented to try to maintain a kind of order.

People were encouraged to get married because it was normal.

They were encouraged to work because it was normal. They were put into factories and lived round the factories and drank in the pubs to anaesthetise themselves from the wretched bloody misery of the life in the factories because that was the normal thing to do.

I'm not worried about him because he's not normal. I'm worried about you because I think you're going to do something you regret.

Susan   I'm not.

Isaac   I know you Susan.

Susan   You bloody don't.

Isaac   There's nothing more horrible than watching your children make mistakes. You want to get inside their bodies and make the correct decision for them. You can't.

Susan   I have no interest at all in getting inside her body.

Isaac   She has to do some things that she'll regret.

Susan   She reminds me of Ted. She makes me think about him. I hate it.

Isaac   Why do you hate that?

Susan   I was angry enough with him when he was alive but that's nothing compared to how angry I am with him for going and flipping well dying on me.

I wish he was here. He'd tell me what to do.

Isaac He wouldn't. He wouldn't have noticed.

Susan He'd be better than you are. You just stand there. You never actually do anything, do you. You don't know me one bit. He knew me.

I worry about Ruthy.

Isaac She's not yours to worry about.

Susan She may as well be.

Isaac Susan.

Susan I look after her more than she does.

Isaac That's not true.

Susan You're soft. That's your problem.

Isaac I'm not.

Susan You're stupid.

You'd do anything for me wouldn't you? You always would have done. Don't think I never realised that because I did.

Tell me I'm wrong.

See.

I'm sorry. You're just about the world's nicest man you aren't you?

Isaac Not in any way.

Cathy *enters.*

Cathy Mum. Mum. Mum. Hiya. Hi Isaac.

Isaac Hello lovely. How are you?

Cathy I'm really absolutely and totally brilliant.

Isaac Gosh.

Cathy I know. How are you Isaac?

Isaac I'm great love.

Cathy How's work?

Isaac It's exactly the same as it always is.

Cathy Hair's still hair is it?

Isaac Hair is still hair.

Cathy Where's Ruthy?

Susan She's asleep.

Cathy How's she been?

Susan She's been lovely.

Cathy Has she been asleep all day?

Susan No. She was awake until about twenty minutes ago. She's been ever so playful. She's been smiling away.

Cathy Has she?

Susan She's started smiling when she sees me. I think she recognises me.

Cathy She smiles at anything her. She smiles at lamp-posts.

Susan She's a happy little soul.

Isaac Susan. Cathy. I should be getting off.

Cathy Don't go I only just got here.

Isaac I have to. I've got to get up early tomorrow. I need to get some dinner. I need to do an order for the shop. I'm really sorry.

Cathy I got a B for my coursework essay.

Isaac Cathy that's brilliant.

Cathy It's the best grade I've ever got. Mr Lewis told me it was the most sophisticated essay I'd written yet. It's about the causes and consequences of the Paris Commune.

Isaac Blimey.

Susan   What the blazes is the Paris Commune?

Isaac   It was a municipal government set up in Paris in 1871.

Susan   It was a what?

Cathy   Like a council.

Isaac   It was the first time the working classes had ever held any kind of political power. It was an amazingly significant time. It was brought down in a bloodthirsty battle. Tens of thousands of people were killed. They were shot up against the walls of Père Lachaise Cemetery in Paris.

Cathy   I was basically arguing that it was all their own fault.

Isaac   Were you?

Cathy   They were asking for it. If people don't live in order and sense then all you get is chaos. That was my main argument.

Isaac   Was it?

Cathy   Mr Lewis said that I was wrong but he liked my essay because I was so passionate about it.

Isaac   I can't believe you thought the Paris Commune deserved to be crushed. Mr Lewis is right to tell you you're wrong. I'm as appalled as I am proud. And I'm very, very late.

Cathy   Stay for a bit.

Isaac   I can't.

Cathy   You can.

Isaac   Thank you. I can't. I'll come back. I'm dead proud of you. A B!

Cathy   I know.

Isaac   Look after your mother.

Cathy   I always do.

Isaac   Look after your daughter.

Susan   As if I had any choice in the matter.

Isaac   Give Ruth a kiss from me.

Cathy   Okay.

Isaac   I'll see you soon ladies. Have a glorious evening.

Cathy   Bye Isaac.

Isaac   Bye.

Susan   Bye Isaac.

Isaac   See you soon Susan. It was lovely to see you.

He leaves.

Cathy   How long's he been here?

Susan   All afternoon. Looking at me. With his big stupid eyes.

Cathy   You should just marry him Mum.

Susan   I'm going to ignore that.

Cathy   You'd make a lovely couple you two. You should get engaged. Susan Berg's got a lovely ring to it, I think.

Susan   You're being stupid Cathy.

Cathy   I'm not. I'm just happy.

Susan   What on earth have you got to be happy about all of a sudden?

Cathy   Life. Getting a B. Seeing Isaac. Coming home. College as a whole.

Susan   I see.

Cathy   I'm really enjoying it at the moment. The other students are starting to understand me. They're starting to enjoy my company. Mr Lewis is lovely. He's a strange old man and he smells of pipes but he's really sweet and very encouraging and I've made a decision.

Susan   Have you?

Cathy   I have yeah.

Susan   What have you decided now?

Cathy   I have decided that I think I would like to carry on studying History and maybe go to polytechnic.

Mr Lewis was talking about it to me yesterday. He was telling me about Canterbury Polytechnic.

Susan   Canterbury?

Cathy   He said that Canterbury Polytechnic was an excellent place to look into the study of History for somebody who doesn't have as many qualifications as you might need to get into universities or somewhere like that.

Susan   Are you being sarcastic?

Cathy   No. I'm being serious. It's as good as a lot of recognised university qualifications he said and I was thinking that what I could do if everything goes well is that I could maybe look at training to be a teacher. Perhaps at primary. Perhaps at secondary. Maybe at nursery school level.

Susan   Cathy. You're not exactly university material are you sweetheart.

Cathy   John thinks it's a great idea.

Susan   Does he?

Cathy   He's proud of me he said. He said he'd definitely be happy to leave Stockport and come and find somewhere in Canterbury to stay.

Susan   I bet he did.

Cathy   It's such a beautiful town. Parts of Canterbury Cathedral date from the seventh century. I bet you didn't know that did you?

Susan   What would you do with Ruth?

Cathy   We'd take her with us.

Susan   You couldn't do that.

Cathy   Course we could. You could come and visit us. It's in Kent. It's beautiful. It's not even that far from the sea. She'd love that. She loves the seaside.

Susan   Who'd look after her?

Cathy   I would. John would. We'd take it in turns.

Susan   John?

Cathy   He's great with her. He's ever so gentle. We could maybe get a nanny if John finds a job in accountancy, which is what he wants to do. Mr Kirkby is really pleased with him. He's going to set him up for accountancy exams in the summer he said.

Susan   John can't look after Ruthy.

Cathy   He can. There'd probably be a play school at the college anyway because they have to provide them now. It's part of the laws.

Susan   There is no way John Connolly is looking after my grand-daughter.

Pause. **Cathy** *stops. She looks at* **Susan***.*

Cathy   What?

Susan   There isn't.

Cathy   Don't be silly.

Susan   I'm not being silly. You're being silly. I won't allow it. He's not allowed to.

Cathy   Not allowed to? What do you mean he's not allowed to? Who are you to go round starting telling people what they are and what they're not allowed to do. Blimey Mum, who do you think you are all of a sudden.

Susan   I didn't want to do this.

Cathy   You what?

Susan   I really didn't.

Cathy   What are you jibber jabbering on about now?

Susan   There's something I need to tell you love.

Cathy   Is there?

Susan   It's about John.

Cathy   Is it?

Susan   I think he's having an affair with Siobhan Hennessey.

Cathy   Do you?

Susan   I think he is in love with her.

Cathy   Well that's a surprise. Coming from you. Honestly Mum you should see how your brain works some of the time.

Susan   I saw them.

Cathy   Oh yeah?

Susan   I went round to your flat to leave some milk because I'd popped off to the grocer's and I'd got more than I needed and I was passing by yours and he was in there and he tried his hardest to stop me coming in because she was in there with him but I saw her and she was in there with him and she was wearing your dressing gown. She was. I'm sorry.

Cathy   When was this?

Susan   On Monday.

Cathy   It can't have been on Monday. We went to Blackpool on Monday Mum. You must have made a mistake. You must have got it wrong.

Susan   I didn't.

Cathy   You must have seen somebody else.

Susan   It wasn't.

Cathy   How can he have been at her flat if he was in Blackpool? Think about it. Use your fucking brain Mum please.

Susan   Don't swear at me young lady.

Cathy   I'm only swearing because I'm exasperated by what an idiot you're being and how mental you are and how stupid you are. That's the only reason I'm swearing.

Susan   It was in the morning. Before you brought Ruthy round.

Cathy   He was at work in the morning.

Susan   Ring Mr Kirkby.

Cathy   What?

Susan   Ring him now and ask him if John was at work in the morning on Monday?

Cathy   No. I'm not going to do that because it would mean I was taking you seriously and I'm sorry I'm just not.

Susan   Sweetheart.

Cathy   Don't sweetheart me. I'm not your sweetheart. I'm John's sweetheart. I'm his fiancée.

Susan   You're what?

Cathy   We're getting married.

He took me to Blackpool beach and sat me down in the moonlight and asked me to marry him. It was the most romantic thing on earth so don't start making all kinds of lies about him because that would be horrible and unfair and untrue.

Susan   You can't.

Cathy   I can.

Susan   After everything I've done for you and Ruthy. After all the things I had to put up with.

Cathy   Blah blah blah blah blah blah blah.

Susan   I knew this was going to happen.

Cathy   Blah blah blah.

Susan   I always knew this was the kind of thing you would do. I could tell it from the moment you were born.

Cathy   Blah blah blah.

Susan   When you were born I screamed at all the doctors to take you away cause you were ugly as anything and even then I could tell you were broken.

I tried getting shot of you and I couldn't. I tried smothering you but I couldn't go through with it. I did think about selling you but nobody wanted to buy you. I should have tried harder is what I should have done. I should have left you on the bloody doorstep somewhere.

Ring him.

Cathy   No.

Susan   Ring him.

Cathy   No.

Susan   Ring him.

Cathy *leaves.* **Susan** *is left alone on stage. She looks all around herself as though not recognising her own flat.*

Cathy *comes back.*

Susan   What did he say? What did he say Cathy?

Cathy   I need to go.

Susan   What did he say love?

Cathy   I need to find John.

Susan   I thought you said he was at work. What did Mr Kirkby say?

Cathy   If I go and find John will you look after Ruthy?

Susan   No.

Cathy   What?

Susan   I can't.

Cathy   What?

Susan   I can't sweetheart. I'm busy.

Cathy   What are you talking about busy?

Susan   I'm sorry love.

Cathy   What are you sorry for?

Susan   I know what it's like.

Cathy   You don't.

Susan   Your father was the same.

Cathy   He wasn't.

Susan   By the time he finally told me what he'd been doing I couldn't do anything about it because of you. Can you imagine if you'd had a baby with him? That would have been unbearable. Wouldn't it?

Cathy   Shut up.

Susan   It's okay. I don't mind if you tell me to shut up. Because what I'm telling you is the complete truth.

Cathy   I don't know what to do Mum.

Susan   When he gets back tonight tell him what you found out and that you're going to come back here and live with me.

Cathy   I can't do that.

Susan   You can.

Cathy   I'd look pretty stupid if I did though wouldn't I? It has to be a bit more than that doesn't it.

Susan   What do you mean?

Cathy   I can't just let him get away with treating me like this and just come home and pretend it never happened.

Susan   What are you talking about?

Cathy   I'm going to have to do something a bit more than that Mum, don't you think?

Susan   What do you mean a bit more than that?

Cathy   You know. Dad knows. You know what I mean.

Yeah. You're right. She is a bit.

She moves to leave.

Susan   Cathy where are you going?

Cathy   I'm going to find John. I'm going to sort this out.

Susan   What about Ruthy?

Cathy   Don't call her Ruthy. Her name's Ruth. I'm the only one who's allowed to call her Ruthy, Mum you know that.

All of a sudden I feel an awful lot better. Do you ever get a feeling like that?

Susan   Like what?

Cathy   When everything, all of a sudden, is very, very clear.

Scene Nine

Isaac's shop. **Isaac** *and* **Cathy**. **Cathy** *has Ruthy with her in a buggy. She pushes her back and forth as she talks.* **Isaac** *enjoys watching them.*

Cathy   Will you do me a favour?

Isaac   Course I will poppet.

Cathy   How do you know? I've not even asked you what it is yet.

Isaac   You don't need to. I'd do anything for you.

Cathy   Are you sure?

Isaac   I was. I'm getting a bit nervous now.

Cathy   Nervous?

Isaac   I can't help feeling that I've agreed to something a bit prematurely.

Cathy (*about the shop*)   You're quiet.

Isaac   It hasn't been. This is my first break.

Cathy   Are your fingers all sore from cutting haircut after haircut after haircut?

Isaac   A little. Maybe. No.

Cathy   Don't you get bored of asking people about their holidays?

Isaac   I don't ask people about their holidays.

Cathy   No actually thinking about it I don't suppose you do.

Isaac   I like people.

Cathy   I noticed.

Isaac   They're underestimated actually.

Cathy   Do you think so?

Isaac   People like that harridan Thatcher build up whole mythologies about people being selfish and untrustworthy and greedy and corrupt and they're not. They're all right. What's the favour?

Cathy   What's a harridan?

Isaac   It's an eighteenth-century word for a large, worn-out horse.

Cathy   Isaac.

Isaac   Cathy.

Cathy   Are you in love with my Mum?

Isaac   Am I what?

Cathy   You're always round at our house. You look at her with your big old droopy old eyes. You might as well tell me. I bet she'd definitely marry you if you wanted her to.

Isaac   Cathy. I am not in love with your mother. I love her very much. But Ted was my closest friend and I could never really get over that.

She examines him for a while, smiles at this idea.

Cathy   I don't believe you. I think you're just scared of what would happen if you did what you really wanted to do most of all in all the world.

I think that's why you talk about politics all the time. As a distraction.

What was he like?

Isaac   What do you mean?

Cathy   You never really know your parents until you get well into being an adult and I never had that opportunity with him. What kind of friend was he?

Isaac   He was very loyal. He was very funny. He could be a bit bonkers too, like you. I loved him.

I was six when I met him. The month I first came to Stockport. 1943. He was in my class. He never asked me any embarrassing questions about where I came from or about Germany or what happened there or anything like that. He was my mate ever since. That's about the sum of it.

Cathy   It's funny.

Isaac   What?

Cathy   Imagining your dad as somebody's mate. Will you take Johnny out for me? Buy him a pint.

Isaac   Why?

Cathy   I think he could do with a good wise talking to. And I want him out of the house tonight. I'm planning a treat for him.

Isaac   That's nice.

Cathy   He really likes you, you know?

Isaac   Does he?

Cathy   He said he sometimes thought you were trying to own me but he liked your calmness and your wisdom.

Isaac   I see.

Cathy   Will you?

Isaac   Won't he be a bit shocked, if I just turn up on his doorstep and offer to buy him a pint?

Cathy   Yeah. But he quite likes shocks. Did you hear that he slept with Shiv?

He stares at her.

That was why I thought he needed a good wise conversation.

Isaac   Cathy, are you okay?

Cathy   I am. I'm fine. I just want you to talk to him.

Isaac   I am so sorry.

Cathy   Don't be.

Isaac   Do you mind if I call him a fucking toe-ragged shit?

Cathy   No.

Isaac   He's a fucking toe-ragged shit.

Cathy   I know. I've decided I'm going to punish him.

I came up with a brilliant idea. I can't tell you what it is
because it'd really surprise you and you'd probably try and
stop me or you'd tell the police and then things would just
go from bad to worse.

Isaac   Cathy why would I tell the police?

Cathy   You wouldn't really. But I bet you'd try and stop me
and I've got this smashing idea and it'd really annoy him
and don't you think he deserves to be annoyed? All you need
to do is go and get him from his flat and say you've heard
what's happened and you just want to talk to him and tell
him you're not angry and you promise you'll buy him a pint
and let him sort his head out and then when he comes back
he'll get the shock of his life.

Here.

Isaac   What?

She gives him a long, lingering kiss.

Cathy   Was that nice?

I knew you'd like it. I bet you've been wondering about that
for years and years.

Isaac   Cathy.

Cathy   Do you feel morally compromised now? See. You've
got to do my favour for me.

You're funny. Your face. Are you a bit shocked?

Isaac   No.

Cathy   Are you a little bit excited? I can tell. There are ways
in which boys reveal themselves. Don't judge me.

Isaac   I'm not.

Cathy   Do you promise me not to judge me?

Isaac   Cathy calm down.

Cathy   You have the most beautiful hands. One day will you cut my hair?

Isaac   What? Er. Yes. Okay.

Cathy   Don't really. I was only joking. You'd make a right mess of it I bet.

Eight o'clock. My house. Don't let me down. Will you?

Scene Ten

Siobhan's *flat.* **Siobhan** *and* **Cathy**. *Ruthy is with her in the buggy.* **Cathy** *pays slightly less attention to her.*

Cathy   Hiya.

Siobhan   How did you get in?

Cathy   I'm really sorry. It was dead easy. Your lock's really simple to break through. I hope you don't mind. I was waiting for you ages. I was just passing by. I had something to give you and I thought you'd be in but you weren't so I waited for twenty minutes and there was still no sign and it was getting a little bit chilly for Ruthy and I was getting a bit bored so I thought I'd just pop the lock.

Siobhan   You popped the lock?

Cathy   It's not damaged. There's a trick. John taught me. You look really cross. Are you really cross?

Siobhan   No. No. No. No. I'm a bit confused.

Cathy   Yeah. It must be a bit surprising.

Siobhan   It is.

Cathy   I didn't mean to make you cross.

Siobhan   You haven't.

Cathy I have, you little liar. I should have called. If I'd called I would have known you were going out. I never think about these things. I just blinking well do the first thing that pops into my mind. Is this a really bad time or something?

Siobhan No. No. You nana. It's fine. You don't need to call. You idiot. It's just a bit unusual.

Cathy Yeah. And it is a bit rude too though, isn't it? Just turning up. Out of the blue. Do you want a cup of tea? The kettle's on.

Siobhan No thank you.

Cathy You sure?

Siobhan I am yeah. I'm totally sure.

Cathy Do you want a drink or something?

Siobhan No. Honestly I'm fine.

Cathy You've got a bottle of flipping gin in there I noticed. We could have gin and tonics. I didn't know you drank gin. Have you ever broken into anybody's house?

Siobhan No.

Cathy It's dead easy. Would you like me to show you? No don't worry. I don't have to. It's a bit of a trade secret. I should probably keep it to myself. How are you?

Siobhan I'm great. How are you?

Cathy I'm great too.

Siobhan That's good.

Cathy I know. Where've you been?

Siobhan At work.

Cathy Have you?

Siobhan Yeah.

Cathy   Have you really?

Siobhan   Er, yeah.

Cathy   You're not being a bit of a cheeky Charlie lying chops?

Siobhan   No. I'm still in my uniform.

Cathy   Oh yeah. I didn't notice. How was it, work?

Siobhan   Boring.

Cathy   Was it?

Siobhan   Yeah.

Cathy   It's horrible when it's boring isn't it?

Siobhan   You're telling me.

Cathy   Hey.

Siobhan   What?

Cathy   Guess what?

Siobhan   What?

Cathy   I skived off!

Siobhan   Did you?

Cathy   Yeah. It was brilliant.

Siobhan   I wish I'd done that.

Cathy   I know. I've never done it before. I didn't know it'd be so easy. I just rang up. Told them I had food poisoning.

You can't in the food industry when somebody says they have food poisoning you can't allow them to come into work on account of cross-contamination. Are you sure you don't want a gin?

Siobhan   No. I'm fine. Honestly. How's Ruthy?

Cathy   Oh you know.

Siobhan Yeah.

Cathy Exhausting.

Siobhan Yeah.

Cathy A bit annoying.

Siobhan Yeah.

Cathy Still crying all the time. Not right now.

Siobhan No. How's John coping with that?

Cathy He's coping just brilliantly. He's so lovely with her. He lets me sleep through the night. He just says 'you go to sleep love, I'll sort her out'. He told me he loved her more than he loved me. I got dead jealous. Not really. I'm so lucky.

Siobhan You are.

Cathy And I didn't tell you; he's doing amazing at work.

Siobhan Is he?

Cathy Mr Kirkby told him he was an 'outstanding' apprentice. He said that he's been employing apprentices for years and years and he'd never seen someone work so hard or be so accomplished. It's amazing when you think about it.

Siobhan That's great Cathy.

Cathy I know. And guess what else.

Siobhan What else?

Cathy You'll never guess this one.

Siobhan What?

Cathy If I tell you do you promise not to laugh?

Siobhan Okay.

Cathy He asked me to marry him.

Siobhan Did he?

Cathy   No. Sorry. That was wrong. I asked him to marry me and he said yes. So we're going to get married. I am so definitely changing my name by the way. I'm not bothered about all these women libbers. I am definitely going to be Cathy Connolly. I'm going to change Ruthy's name too. So she'll be Ruth Connolly and then we're going to try to sort out an official adoption. So John'll be her father because if anything happened then she'd actually have to go and live with my mum and I don't really want her to do that.

Siobhan   Don't you?

Cathy   No.

Siobhan   How come?

Cathy   I don't think I trust her.

Siobhan   What do you mean?

Cathy   I think she might tell a few lies every now and then a few pork pies.

Did you never get that sense off her?

Siobhan   No.

Cathy   Gosh. I did. She's going fucking doolally.

Siobhan   That's amazing news Cathy.

Cathy   I know. I'm so excited.

Siobhan   When was this?

Cathy   On Monday night. In the moonlight. On Blackpool beach.

Siobhan   Oh come here. I'm so pleased for you. He's really lovely and he's dead fit and you two make a lovely couple and it's just the best news ever.

Cathy   Thank you. So. I wanted to ask you.

Siobhan   What?

Cathy   I hope you're not going to be annoyed.

Siobhan   Why? What do you want to ask me?

Cathy   Nothing. Well. Something. Nothing much. I found this.

Siobhan   What?

Cathy   Here. I was getting changed this morning and I found this and I'd not worn it for ages and I tried it on and it's lovely but it doesn't fit me any more at all. I must have put on weight or something. It must be John. He must be feeding me up. Like his little piggy. And I didn't want to throw it away and John likes me with a little bit of flesh on me so I don't want to go on a diet or anything so I thought what I'd do was pop over here and see if you wanted it and let you have it. And I came round and you weren't in. So I popped your lock, which in one way is a bit naughty but in another way at least you know now. You'd better change your locks hadn't you? Anyway. Here.

She passes the dress that she was wearing in Scene Two to **Siobhan**. *It is wrapped in paper.* **Siobhan** *unwraps it. She holds it up. It is beautiful.*

Siobhan   Thank you.

Cathy   What do you think?

Siobhan   I'm a bit taken aback. This is a bit overwhelming.

Cathy   Is it?

Siobhan   You being here. And all your news. This is all –

Cathy   What do you think about the dress?

Siobhan   I think it's lovely.

Cathy   Do you?

Siobhan   I remember you wearing this.

Cathy   I've not worn it for years.

Siobhan Are you sure?

Cathy Totally sure.

Siobhan But it looks really lovely on you.

Cathy It doesn't fit me anymore.

Siobhan Cathy. Thank you.

Cathy Don't be silly. It's only a dress. Don't go overboard. Oh my God.

Siobhan What?

Cathy I just realised. Did you think I was going to ask you to be my bridesmaid? I really set you up for that didn't I? I wasn't even thinking.

Siobhan I didn't think that.

Cathy I've not even started thinking about that. We've not even talked about it. I just came round to give you my dress.

Siobhan No. Silly. It didn't even cross my mind.

Cathy I bet it did and you're being all humble and lovely.

Siobhan It didn't.

Cathy I bet it did.

Siobhan Should I go and try it on?

Cathy Yeah.

Siobhan Can you stay here for a bit?

Cathy Yeah. I'll make a cup of tea.

I might make myself a gin and tonic.

Siobhan It's totally lovely. Thank you. Wait here.

Cathy *is left alone. She starts crying hysterically. Silently. She starts hitting her own head and pinching her own arms. She stops. She pulls herself together.*

Siobhan   What do you think?

Cathy   It's beautiful.

Siobhan   I love it.

Cathy   It's such a lovely colour with your hair.

Siobhan   It's really lovely Cathy. Thank you.

Cathy   You're my best friend Shiv. It's only a dress you nana.

Siobhan   Well I love it. It's really kind of you.

Cathy   Good. I'm glad you're happy. You'd better agree to be my bridesmaid now when I do get round to asking you when we've sorted everything out.

Siobhan   Course I will. Come here.

They have a big hug.

Did you get a cup of tea?

Cathy   I didn't, no.

Siobhan   Do you want one?

Cathy   No thank you. I've changed my mind.

Siobhan   Did you want that gin and tonic? I could have one with you.

We could have a celebration. This doesn't happen every day does it?

Cathy   I don't want one. I'm fine. Can I say?

Siobhan   What?

Cathy   There's something I can't figure out.

Siobhan   What do you mean?

Cathy   I've been thinking my hardest and looking back over my calendar and everything and I can't quite put my finger on it.

Siobhan On what?

Cathy When was, right, when was the first time you had sex with Johnny, Shiv?

Silence.

Was it on Monday or was it before that?

Siobhan What are you talking about?

Cathy I know you had sex with him on Monday morning before we went to Blackpool.

Siobhan I didn't.

Cathy You did, didn't you? Didn't you Shiv? Mum saw you. She told me.

Siobhan Your mum?

Cathy Was it last week?

How long was it after you'd met him? Was it a week? Two weeks? A day? Was it something very impulsive? Did it just crop up in conversation or had you planned it for ages and ages?

What's the matter? Has the cat got your tongue?

I should set you on fire or something shouldn't I? You're meant to be my best friend. The least you could do is tell me when it was couldn't you? Is that an unreasonable thing to ask?

Siobhan Cathy I'm so sorry.

Cathy Why?

Siobhan I'm so sorry. I didn't mean to. I had no idea. He – he – he – he –

Cathy He what? He what Shiv what did he do? He didn't rape you or anything did he?

Siobhan No.

Cathy   Phew. That's a relief. Imagine how horrible it would be if he had!

Siobhan   He didn't.

Cathy   Are you completely in love with him? Shiv.
Answer me.

Have you fallen in love with John?

Siobhan   Cathy.

Cathy   It's funny. You think you know somebody and then you find out something and it makes you want to cut their cheeks off with their kitchen scissors or grind glass into their eyes or something like that. It makes you really want to hurt them. I won't. Don't worry. But don't think I don't want to with all of my heart because I completely and totally do. I have so caught you by surprise haven't I? Can I warn you, from this moment on you'd better watch your back. You'd better leave Stockport. If I was you I'd leave England altogether. I'd run away and keep running because no matter how far you get it won't be far enough and no matter where you go I will never, ever, never stop following you.

Scene Eleven

John's *flat*. **John** *and* **Cathy**. *She pushes the buggy with her. She seems more disconnected from it than ever.*

John   Cathy?

She looks at him and doesn't respond.

What are you doing here?

She looks at him and doesn't respond.

I thought you were at work. I thought I was going to get some time to myself.

She looks at him and doesn't respond.

How's Ruthy?

She looks at him and doesn't respond.

Is she okay?

Are you all right? You look like you've seen a ghost.

Cathy   Why aren't you at work?

John   Mr Kirkby said I could leave early. I like your dress. I've not seen that before, have I?

Cathy   I don't know.

Do you know something I've only just noticed about you?

John   What?

Cathy   Your aura.

John   My what?

Cathy   It's a very unusual colour.

John   Is it? What is it?

Cathy   Ruthy must be able to see it. That's one of the things that babies can do. It's why she notices you. It's a violent colour. It's horrible.

Don't do that.

John   Do what?

Cathy   Don't give me that look.

John   Cathy you're being quite strange.

Cathy   You make me feel so proud. I see people watching you walk down the street and I think 'he's my boyfriend'. And now you do this to me.

John   Do what to you?

Cathy   I was talking to my mum. She told me she saw you.

John   Which she must have enjoyed.

Cathy On Monday morning.

John Whereabouts?

Cathy Ha. Good mind games. Good idea John. Play your little funny magic tricks.

John What magic tricks? What are you talking about magic tricks? I was at work on Monday morning.

Cathy She saw what you did.

John You're talking entirely in riddles you lunatic.

Cathy With my best friend. Fucking her.

She did, John, don't try and deny it because if you try and deny it I'll pick something really heavy up and smash it into the back of your head.

Silence.

He stares at her.

She moves closely to him. She unbuttons a button on his shirt. He is frozen to the spot.

Do you know sometimes I do think we are on the edge of the world and that judgement day is coming and everything is awful and we're really going to get it? We're really in an awful lot of trouble. I've never told anybody that before but I really think it is the case. I do. I do. I do. I do.

I really. I did. I really. I trusted you.

Do you know how hard it is for me to introduce men to Ruthy? It's not easy John. It's really, I love her so much. But I thought with you there could be –

I would do anything for you. I really don't think that you would do anything for me in the same way. Do you believe me? Because I will prove it. I will. I will. I love you more than I love her and you did that to me and it makes me want to.

John I didn't do anything. She's lying.

Cathy   I told you not to deny it. I don't believe you just denied it when I told you really clearly not to.

John   Cathy, your mum is lying to you. It's what mothers do, Cathy. Believe me I fucking know mate.

Cathy   Everything's gone backwards. This whole country's gone upside down. The good things are bad things the bad things are good things.

John   Cathy, please.

Cathy   Be quiet.

John   I'm getting a little bit unnerved I have to confess.

Cathy   You fucking coward.

I called Mr Kirkby. He said you'd not been in work for two weeks.

John   You called him?

Cathy   I can't believe I didn't notice.

John   You spoke to Mr Kirkby behind my back?

He looks at her.

Do you remember what your life was like before you met me? Living in your pissy little house with your pissy little mother. Waddling around Reddish Road with your pissy little friend. Waiting for buses. Admiring the beauty of Reddish Vale. I gave you a universe of opportunity and don't think I didn't because I did.

What is it with women? The only good woman I ever met in the whole world is Ruthy.

He looks at her.

John   It was one fuck. It didn't mean anything.

She hits him hard across his face. She gasps in excitement.

I swear to Christ Cathy Heyer if you lay one more finger on me ever again I will fucking brain you so help me God I will.

Cathy   It's nothing compared to what I'm going to do.

John   What do you mean?

Cathy   Have a guess. No. You'll never be able to.

He looks at her.

John   Are you crying? I've never seen you cry before. You don't cry.

Don't. Cathy. Don't cry.

I feel awful now.

Cathy   Fuck off.

John   Here.

He wipes a tear away from her eye with a thumb.

Cathy   Don't.

John   Real tears!

Cathy   Please John, don't.

John   Your mother. What is she like? We'll go and talk to her. The crazy old cunt. Both of us. I'll hold your hand.

Cathy   John. Don't. Don't. Don't. Don't.

John   I bet I can make you smile.

Scene Twelve

John's *flat.* **Cathy** *and Ruthy. Ruthy is in her cot. She is silent.* **Cathy** *approaches her. She stops. Hears something. Looks up.*

Cathy   Water and shit and skin and bone. She's not real. She's made out of rubber.

She holds up Ruthy's pillow. She smells it.

Look at you.

Imagine growing up as you?

Scene Thirteen

Susan's *bedroom.*

Susan *is asleep in bed.* **Cathy** *sits on her bed brushing her hair.*
Brushing and brushing and brushing it.

Susan   Cathy?

Cathy   Did I wake you up?

Susan   What are you doing?

Cathy   I'm sorry. I tried my hardest to be really quiet.

Susan   What are you doing love?

Cathy   I'm brushing my hair. Do you think if I brush it
hard enough it'll grow back?

Susan   What are you doing here, I meant?

Cathy   I'm sorry. I honestly didn't mean to wake you.

Susan   It's quarter to five in the morning love.

Cathy   I know. I'm sorry.

Susan   What's wrong sweetheart?

Cathy   Nothing.

Susan   Why aren't you at John's?

Cathy   Have you seen how sunny it is?

Susan   Did you tell him?

Cathy   I love it when days start like this. It's like something
magical's happening I think.

Susan   Did you tell John, Cathy?

Did you tell him what I told you?

Cathy *smiles at her.*

Susan   What are you smiling about?

Cathy   I'm just happy.

Susan   It's nice. I'm just not used to seeing you smile.
You've got a lovely smile.

Cathy   Thank you.

Susan   It's just a bit of a surprise waking up and finding
you here.

Cathy   It must be.

Susan   Are you okay?

Cathy   I'm fine.

Susan   What did he say?

Cathy   Who?

Susan   John.

Cathy   John who?

Susan   Your John.

Cathy   You'd better ask him hadn't you? I wasn't really
listening to be honest.

Susan   Was he very cross?

Cathy   Not really he wasn't. He just kept going on and on
and on. It was very irritating.

Susan   Have you come back home now?

Cathy   Mum. Can I ask you something?

Susan   Go on.

Cathy   How are you?

Susan   What do you mean how am I?

Cathy   Can I get you a cup of tea?

Susan   It's a bit early for a cup of tea love.

Cathy   Is it?

Susan   It is a bit poppet yeah. How did you get into
the house?

Cathy   I used my key. I'm not exactly gonna break in am I?

Susan   No. Sorry. Do you want to get in here with me?

Cathy   Maybe. That'd be nice. Thank you. We've not done
this for ages have we?

Susan   No.

Cathy   It's nice.

Susan   I like it. Cathy.

Cathy   Yeah.

Susan   I'm really sorry.

Cathy   What about?

Susan   About what I said earlier. About saying I didn't
want you.

Cathy   That's okay.

Susan   It wasn't true.

Cathy   Wasn't it?

Susan   Of course it wasn't. I just get so angry sometimes. I
don't mean to.

Cathy   It's all right. I'm not cross.

Susan   Aren't you?

Cathy   I don't blame you for saying things like that to
be honest.

Susan   Don't you?

Cathy   I don't blame you for anything. It wasn't your fault.

We're just the least lucky girls in all the world. All three of us.
You and me and Ruthy have been given a big sad spoon of
bad luck.

We should have a dance us two.

Susan   You what?

Cathy   We should. I like a nice dance.

Susan   Are you all right sweetheart?

Cathy   I am Mum, yeah. I'm fine.

Susan   Is Ruthy okay?

Cathy   She is now, yeah.

Susan   Where is she? Where is she Cathy?

Cathy   Ssshhh.

Susan   What?

Cathy   You. You have to be quiet.

Susan   Why?

Cathy   You can't tell.

Susan   What do you mean?

Cathy   If I tell you a secret do you promise to keep it?

Susan   What is it?

Cathy   Do you promise you're not going to tell?

Susan   Okay.

Cathy   Do you swear?

Susan   Okay. I swear. What is it?

Cathy   I killed her.

I killed Ruthy.

I smothered her with a pillow when she was asleep. Is that awful?

It's a good job you promised not to tell isn't it?

Can you imagine if I hadn't made you promise. This would be really embarrassing. I'd get in so much trouble. Are you a bit shocked? Your face is a right picture.

Susan   What are you talking about Cathy?

Cathy   I did. I left her in her cot at John's flat. I did it on purpose so that he'd have to find her. I smothered her. She was fast asleep. She didn't feel a thing.

What?

What's wrong?

Susan   Are you lying?

Cathy   No. Silly.

Susan   Is this your idea of a joke?

Cathy   No. It's the truth. It wouldn't be a very good joke would it? It wouldn't exactly be a great sense of humour eh?

Susan *stares at her. Some time.*

Susan   You can't have done.

Cathy   I have done.

Susan   You haven't.

Cathy   I have.

Susan   You liar.

Cathy   I'm not lying. Mum calm down.

Susan *looks at her for a time. She gets up out of bed.*

Cathy   Where are you going?

Susan   You're horrible.

Cathy   Where are you going Mum?

Susan   I'm going to go and call John then. Ask him. I'll go round and see him. I'll call the police if I have to and don't think I won't because I will.

Cathy   You look a bit wobbly Mum. You should probably sit down. Your face has gone all white.

Susan   Imagine making something up like that. That's sick is what that is young lady.

Cathy   I didn't make it up.

Susan *stares at her for a long time.*

Cathy   I didn't. Honest.

Susan   Stay there.

Cathy   I wasn't going anywhere.

Susan   Stay right there. Don't touch me.

Cathy   Mum I wasn't going to touch you. I think you're having a bit of a funny turn aren't you.

Susan   You horrible nasty little witch.

Cathy   I'm not a witch.

Susan   Don't try and run away. I'll catch you myself.

Scene Fourteen

Cathy's *prison cell. She is awaiting her verdict.* **Isaac** *is with her. She looks at him. She hits him. He doesn't react. She hits him again and again and again and again. He takes it all. She stops. He goes to rest his hand on her.*

Cathy   Don't touch me.

He stops.

Get your hands off me.

Isaac   I'm sorry.

Cathy   I can't be touched.

Don't.

I want to stand still for a very long time and never move.

Isaac   Cathy they'll come in if you don't calm down.

Cathy   They won't.

Isaac   They're watching us.

Cathy   They're not.

Isaac   They are Cathy. They told me they were.

Cathy   What are you doing here?

Isaac   I came down to wait with you.

Cathy   Who let you in here?

Isaac   The Custody Sergeant said it was okay. He said he thought it was a good idea for somebody to be with you while they're considering their verdict. He said your mum hadn't been.

Cathy   I don't want you here.

Isaac   I'm not going.

A pause.

Cathy   Where's Mum?

Isaac   She's at home.

Cathy   Where's John?

Isaac   I don't know.

Cathy   He's not been in.

Isaac   No.

Cathy   Did he get the shock of his life when he found her? I wish I'd seen his face. I only did it because he liked her so much.

Isaac   I've not seen him.

Cathy   Haven't you?

Isaac   No.

Cathy   Where's he gone?

Isaac   I don't know love.

A pause. She smiles at him.

Cathy   They should bring back hanging and hang me shouldn't they?

Isaac   No.

Cathy   Don't you think that'd be funny?

Isaac   No.

Cathy   Do you not believe in capital punishment?

Isaac   No I don't.

Cathy   Well you should. I do. I sentence me to hang by the neck until I am dead. Do you want a sandwich I've a sudden craving for a sandwich.

Isaac   I'm all right. Would you like me to ask for one for you?

Cathy   In a bit. Yeah.

They look at each other for a while.

Tell John why I did it. I should be enough for him, I think, don't you? I should.

Do you remember when I snogged you? Was that really horrible?

Isaac   No. It wasn't.

Cathy   Do you want me to snog you again?

Isaac   No.

Cathy   They probably wouldn't let us.

Can I tell you Isaac? There is part of me that's quite excited about when she wakes up. Ruthy. I mean I know she won't but I can't wait to see her again. Her eyes always light up when she sees me.

What do you think it'll be like, in prison?

Isaac   I don't know Cathy. I've never been inside a prison before.

Cathy   In primary school, yeah, you line up in pairs and hold your partner's hand. Do you remember that?

Isaac   I do, yes.

Cathy   I sometimes think it would be a nice thing to hold hands more often. Maybe they'll do that in prison.

Did you hear? He was right all along wasn't he? Margaret Thatcher was the winner.

Do you think everything's going to change now?

Isaac   Probably. Yeah. It probably will.

Cathy   A new start.

Isaac   Maybe.

I know what it's like.

Cathy   What, what's like?

Isaac   I know what it feels like to want to do what you did. I know why you did it. I completely understand. I wanted to tell you. I wanted you to know.

Cathy   What are you going on about you eh?

Isaac   It doesn't matter.

Cathy   Have you seen Mum loads and loads?

Isaac   A bit. Not loads and loads.

Cathy   Have you been constantly going round there?

Isaac   No.

Cathy   Do you think Ruthy's in heaven? That's what Mum thinks.

Isaac   I know.

Cathy   Do you think that too?

Isaac   I don't believe in heaven.

Cathy   Don't you? Weirdo.

Isaac   I wish I did.

Cathy   Well then do then.

Isaac   I can't.

Cathy   Yeah you can.

Isaac   I wish I believed in heaven. I wish I believed in God.
I could have been a rabbi by now. I would have made a great
rabbi me. But I don't love. I don't. I just don't.

Part Two

Scene One

The doorway of **Cathy***'s house in Peel in the Isle of Man.* **Cathy** *and* **Harry Connolly***.*

Harry   Cathy Heyer? Is your name Cathy Heyer?

Cathy   No.

Harry   You're Cathy Heyer aren't you?

Cathy   No. I'm not I'm afraid. You must have got the wrong person. How embarrassing. My name's Wendy McGowan.

Harry   That's not true.

Cathy   It is.

Harry   It isn't. It isn't true. You're Cathy Heyer. Aren't you?

Cathy   No. I'm Wendy McGowan.

Harry   If you don't admit to me who you are then I promise you I will knock on every door on this whole street and every door on every street on this whole fucking island I find and I will tell them that you are Cathy Heyer and I'll tell them exactly what you did. Are you Cathy Heyer? Are you Cathy Heyer? This is your last opportunity to answer my question.

Cathy   Who are you?

Harry   My name's Harry Connolly. You knew John Connolly. He's my dad.

Has that come as a bit of a fucking surprise to you? Has it come as a bolt from the fucking blue? It looks like it has. You want to see your face. You don't mind if I don't take my shoes off do you? I didn't think so.

He enters her house.

Cathy   What are you doing here?

Harry   What do you think?

Cathy   I have no idea, that's why I'm asking. How did you get here?

Harry   I got the Manx Ferry to Douglas. I hitch-hiked to Liverpool and got on the first available ferry. It took me nearly twenty-four hours exactly. I haven't slept.

Cathy   Who told you I was here?

Harry   A man called Isaac Berg.

Cathy   I don't believe you.

Harry   I didn't ask you to.

Cathy   He wouldn't tell you.

Harry   He did.

Cathy   He wouldn't tell anybody where I live.

Harry   He told me.

Cathy   He wouldn't do that to me.

Harry   He has done. Sorry.

Cathy   Why would he do that?

Harry   Because I told him how important it was for me to see you. I told him it was part of my therapy. I was lying through my arse and he fucking believed me. I haven't come here for reasons of therapy at all I'm afraid. Don't panic. I'm not going to hurt you. I'd fucking like to, mind you. That's a favourite fucking fantasy of mine that I have properly fucking fantasised about hundreds of fucking times but in the end I'm just a fucking better person than you.

Would you like to hear some of the fantasies I've had about hurting you?

Cathy   No.

Harry   You ruined my dad's life.

Cathy   That's not true.

Harry   He woke up one morning to find a dead baby in his bedroom. That was your fault. Of course it's fucking true. Psychopath.

Cathy   Don't say that.

Harry   Stop me. Killer.

Cathy   Stop it. I'm not a psychopath. Please get out of my house.

Harry   What are you going to do Cathy, scream?

Cathy   If I need to.

Harry   And what the fuck will you tell the neighbours when they fucking get here?

Cathy   Is it strictly necessary for you to swear quite to the extent that you are doing?

Harry   Ha.

Cathy   Why are you laughing?

Harry   Are you judging me? Honestly Cathy I expected a lot of things but I didn't expect a sanctimonious hypocrite.

Cathy   What do you want?

Harry   I want you to know.

Cathy   You want me to what?

Harry   My dad is a fucking wreck. He has been all my life. And I never knew why.

My mum left him when I was four years old and I never knew why.

Two weeks ago he told me what you did to him and all of a
sudden everything made sense. I understood what it was.
That nag. That pull. It had lived in my gut like a rotting
knot and never understood what it was and then I did.

I very much wanted to come and tell you what you've done
and I wanted you to know that I know where you are and
that you can never, ever hide.

Cathy   This is horrible.

Harry   Isaac said you've been living here for a year now is
that true?

Don't they mind you round here or something?

Cathy   What do you mean don't they mind me?

Harry   Do they even know who you are? Because I am
definitely going to tell them.

Cathy   Don't.

Harry   Why not? Why not Cathy? Do you think it's fair that
you get away with it?

Cathy   I'm not. I didn't. I was in jail for sixteen years.

Harry   It's nowhere near long enough. Tell me one good
reason why I shouldn't tell your neighbours who you are?

Cathy   It's nothing to do with them. It's nothing to do
with you.

Harry   Everybody round here thinks you're called Helen.
How the fuck did you think up the name Helen?

Cathy   I don't remember.

Harry   It's stupid. You don't even look like a Helen. Is this
a very friendly community? Is it a jolly little place?

Cathy   Yes it is.

Harry   It's quite fucking retro isn't it? Quite 1950s throw-
back. There are fucking fields fucking everywhere does it
not make you feel a bit sick?

Cathy   No.

Harry   Does everybody all go calling on each other in their funny fucked up cod scouse accents and making each other little cakes and pots of jam and ham sandwiches and presents?

Cathy   No.

Harry   I bet they fucking do.

Cathy   People are just nice to each other.

Harry   What kind of a name for a town is fucking Peel anyway?

Cathy   I think you should go now.

Harry   Do you?

Cathy   If you don't go now I'll call the police.

Harry   Yeah?

Cathy   It's been nice to meet you. It's time for you to go.

Harry   Fucking make me.

Cathy   Don't swear at me. Please go.

Harry   I don't think there's anything wrong with swearing do you Helen Cathy Helen Cathy Helen Cathy?

Cathy   Does he know you're here? Does your father know you're here? Did you tell him you were coming?

How old are you?

Harry   What?

Cathy   How old are you?

Harry   What the fuck has that got to do with you?

Cathy   I didn't know he'd had a child. I didn't even know he got married.

Harry   Yeah funnily enough he didn't invite you. He thought about it and then decided against it partly on account of you serving life imprisonment for murdering a baby and partly on account of the fact that your name made him freeze with fear.

Cathy   Who did he get married to?

Harry   If you honestly think I'm going to tell you that you're even more stupid and fucking mental than I thought.

Cathy   Was it Siobhan Hennessey?

Harry   No it fucking wasn't. Who the fuck is Siobhan Hennessey?

I came here to spit in your face. I came here to kick you or smack you out. I've decided not to do any of those things. But there is something very important that you need to know. I am going to tell you this and then I'm going to leave. You are the worst human being there has ever been. You think you can hide from that? You can't. You think you can change your appearance or your haircut or your clothes or the way you smell or where you live and it'll change anything really? Well you're lying to yourself. You will be found again and again. That was my job. That was what I came here to tell you. Do you understand what I came here to say?

Do you understand what I came here to say?

Do you understand what I came here to say?

Cathy   Yes.

He stares at her for a long time. Picks something up. Looks at it. Puts it down again.

Turns to leave.

Cathy   Where are you going?

Harry   What?

Cathy Where are you going?

Harry That has fucking fuck all to do with you. Psycho.

Cathy You've missed the last ferry.

Harry What?

Cathy And the last plane.

Harry Do you seriously think I give a shit about that?

Cathy Where are you going to stay?

You're going to need to go and get a hotel. Have you got any money for a hotel? There are some quite cheap ones in Douglas or you could get a room in the White Horse or head over to Ramsay. I could lend you some money if you want me to.

You should know that I do have a spare room and I don't mind you staying in it.

Harry Are you fucking joking me?

Cathy No. I'm not. Don't swear.

Harry Are you fucking taking the fucking piss?

Cathy No it's a genuine offer. I mean it quite sincerely. I won't be in any way offended if you'd rather get a hotel but the offer is there.

Harry I'd wake up in the night and cut your throat.

Cathy No you wouldn't.

Harry I fucking would.

Cathy Don't be silly.

Harry I'm not being silly in the fucking least you fucking mental fucking bitch.

Cathy Believe me Harry I've met people who have cut other people's throats. You're absolutely nothing like them whatsoever.

Harry   I'm going.

Cathy   That's absolutely your prerogative.

Harry   I've nothing more to say to you. I have no reason to be here any more.

Scene Two

The top of the hill above Peel Castle. **Cathy** *and* **Harry**. *The next morning.*

Cathy   It's old.

Harry   It looks it.

Cathy   The oldest bits are from the eleventh century.

It was built by Vikings. They found a coffin a few years ago of a woman who was buried in 1050. They called her the Pagan Lady, which I quite liked. It's haunted.

Harry   Shut up.

Cathy   It's haunted by a black dog. It's called the Moddy Dhoo. If you see it you die. You can see seals most days. They come up quite close especially if you sing to them. You can see basking sharks too. They're huge. You can take a boat out to look at them. I've not done that. It's the kind of thing tourists do. I'm glad you stayed. I wanted to ask you something.

Harry   It wasn't out of choice.

Cathy   No.

Harry   I was more embarrassed than I was angry having to come back to you and I was pretty angry.

Cathy   I noticed. How did you sleep?

Harry   How do you think?

Cathy   Have you had enough to eat?

Harry   Yup.

Cathy   You should get an ice cream before you go. The ice cream here is honestly the best ice cream in the world.

What time's your flight?

Harry   4.30.

Cathy   You can get a bus.

Harry   I know.

Cathy   I should have made you a sandwich to take with you. They sell pots of fresh crab in the fishmonger's that are just delicious.

Harry   I don't want a sandwich.

Cathy   No.

Harry   I can get a sandwich on the plane.

Some time.

Cathy   I think I suit living on an island.

It makes me feel safe. I like going for long walks. You can walk all the way around the coast in four days. You get to the top of Snaefell and you can see England, Ireland, Scotland and Wales on a good day. It's 2034 feet high.

We should probably go back down.

Are you really seventeen?

Harry   Yeah.

Cathy   You can't be.

Harry   I am.

Cathy   You don't look seventeen. You look a lot older.

Harry   Fuck off. I'm seventeen.

Cathy   When are you eighteen?

Harry   February 10th.

Cathy   I was seventeen. When I met your dad.

Shouldn't you be at school?

Harry   No.

Cathy   Are you not in sixth form?

Harry   No.

Cathy   Why not? I thought everybody was nowadays.

Harry   I'm not.

Cathy   Why not?

Harry   It's not really any of your business.

Cathy   No. Sorry. I'll figure it out eventually, you know?

Harry   What?

Cathy   I'll figure out why you're not in sixth form eventually. I'll be able to look into your eyes and figure it out.

Harry   You won't.

Cathy   I will. I'm psychic.

He looks at her.

I am. I don't ask you to believe me. I just am.

Harry   You would be.

Cathy   I can see into your mind. I can completely predict your future.

Harry   Magic.

Cathy   I can tell it by reading your aura.

Harry   I could have fucking guessed that.

Cathy   Your aura is particularly brilliant. It's startling.

Harry Fuck off.

Cathy That's why you have to swear so much. It's because you find the energy coursing through your veins on account of your aura being slightly overwhelming so that all you're left able to do is swear and swear and swear. It doesn't really offend me. I say it does but I'm exaggerating. I understand exactly how it feels.

Some time.

Everything you want you will get. Everything you want to achieve you will achieve. Every desire you have you will realise. I can tell.

Don't tell me what they are.

Harry You are really, really weird. And that is me trying my hardest not to swear.

Cathy You will marry Sally one day. You will have two boys. You will take them to the Ancient Pyramids in Cheops. You will live in Germany for a bit. You will one day go skydiving. You will learn to speak another language fluently. You will read all the books you ever wanted to read.

He stares at her.

She smiles back. Struggles not to laugh.

Harry Who told you about Sally?

Cathy Nobody.

Harry How did you know all that?

Cathy Psychic. I told you.

Harry Fucking hell.

Cathy There you go again.

Harry I'm a bit fucking freaked out I have to say.

Cathy Yeah.

Harry   Fuck.

She smiles at him.

Looks away.

Some time.

Cathy   What's she like, Sally?

He can't answer.

Where did you meet her?

Is she your age or is she older than you or younger?

Don't let it worry you.

Just try your hardest to be good to her and then even if you fail she'll like that you tried. Have you got a photograph? Please can I have a look at it?

After a time he takes a photograph out of his pocket and shows it to her.

She's very pretty.

Harry   I know.

Cathy   I don't blame you for being so in love with her. Don't think about what everybody else thinks. It doesn't matter.

Harry   No. What was it you wanted to ask me?

Cathy   It can wait. What time's your bus?

Harry   Not till 3.

Cathy   What are you going to do until then?

Harry   What was my dad like when he was younger?

She looks at him. Some time.

Cathy   One time he took me to Blackpool. We stole a car and just drove up there and walked all along the beach until we were on our own and all you could see was the sea. He

told me he wanted to marry me. He promised that he'd
never take me back home. Every time I hear the word
Blackpool now I think of that night.

He taught me how to rob houses.

Harry   What?

Cathy   Did he never tell you about that?

Harry   Have you gone fucking doolally?

Cathy   It was his favourite pasttime. I'm sorry. He probably
hoped to keep it private. I'm being mean but it is true. He
took me with him a few times. I used to get so nervous. I'd
never broken the law before I met him. It was quite an
exciting feeling. Is that a bit odd to think about?

Harry   Just a bit.

Cathy   Don't you start doing it.

Harry   I don't intend to.

Cathy   That's good.

He never came to the trial. I was cross because I wanted to
see his face. I was sad as well. He always cheered me up. He
had this face he used to pull. You do it too. I've noticed. You
look quite like him.

Harry   I don't.

Cathy   You look like how he used to look.

Harry   I'm nothing like him.

Cathy   No.

People called me a monster in court. I remember having a
moment when I thought that was quite science fiction and I
had to try my hardest not to do a bit of a giggle and I didn't
quite succeed because I just kept seeing him pulling that face
in my head and thinking about what he'd have said and it
just made me laugh.

Some time.

Harry   What was it like being on trial?

Cathy   It was all right.

Harry   Was it?

Cathy   I didn't get nervous or anything if that's what you mean. It was like I was watching somebody else on telly that wasn't actually me at all.

He doesn't answer.

Prison was like that too. When they first took us there the sounds and the size of the gates and the walls all looked very familiar because I'd seen them so much on telly. It was like being taken onto a television set. It's the smell that makes you realise at first. Prison smells of cabbage and urine. I know that now but when I first smelt it I was a bit taken aback.

I changed.

The first day they took me to Staffordshire I sat on a concrete slab and they hosed me down to get rid of all the nits and the infection and it was exactly at that moment then that I changed. My whole body changed. I became a different person with a different body. It was the saddest feeling ever but in the end it was all okay. It's a shame it didn't happen earlier. If I'd been a different person I wouldn't have done the things that I did.

She sucks her thumb.

Harry   What was it like?

Cathy   What was what like?

Some time.

It was very quiet. It felt like I was walking away from something horrible and what I wasn't allowed to do was run. She was asleep. She didn't make a noise. I pressed and pressed. It felt like a light going off. It's horrible because it's nothing whatsoever to do with her. It felt like the start of something. I served sixteen years in prison because when I was seventeen I killed my little baby.

What's your mum like?

Harry   Better than he is.

Cathy   What's her name?

Harry   Alison.

Cathy   Alison Connolly?

Harry   Alison Hart, now. She changed her name back.

Cathy   Where did he meet her?

Harry   After he left Stockport he went to live in Portsmouth. He met her there.

It starts to rain.

Cathy   It's raining.

He lifts his face up to the rain to let it pour on his face.

Cathy   What are you doing that for?

Harry   My dad taught me it when I was little.

She can't speak for some time.

Cathy   Do you know what I think?

Harry   No.

Cathy   I think the reason you don't go to sixth form is because of your dad. You think he's graced you with the legacy of not being good enough. It's not true. You are. I think you should go back and do your hardest work. I think you should do the best you possibly can and go and live a life Harry.

Things are changing. The Government's changing. That's one thing. People are starting to realise that we might be all right, and that the country might be all right and that Tony Blair, he might be all right and all. We won't go back to that lot. We won't make that mistake again.

What if this was the beginning of something rather than the end of something? What if in the future they'll look back on this time and think, gosh how primitive and strange and we're not at the end of an adventure we're at the start of it.

Will you tell him you saw me? Harry. Will you tell him you saw me do you think?

Harry   No.

Cathy   Why not?

Harry   If I told him I came here or where you were or that I came to find you he'd never speak to me again. He'd go insane.

Cathy   He wouldn't.

Harry   He would.

Cathy   Tell him.

Harry   No.

Cathy   Tell him you saw me. Please.

Harry   I can't.

Cathy   You so can.

I'd do anything to see him one more time. I loved him so much it hurt my skin. I used to think he was the best thing that ever happened to me. As if by magic the shopkeeper appeared. He changed everything. I think about him every single day. I close my eyes and his face is there behind my eyelids like it's been waiting for me all this time. I can hear his voice and whenever I hear somebody else with the same voice I hold my breath. Tell him that.

Harry   No.

Cathy   Please Harry.

Harry   No.

Cathy   I'll do anything you want me to do.

Harry   I don't want you to do anything. I'm not going to tell him.

Cathy   Hold my hand.

He doesn't.

I'm turning into a bird. If you don't hold my hand Harry I'm worried I might fly away. Am I being a bit mad?

Harry   You are a bit, yeah.

Cathy   I'm sorry.

Can I ask one thing?

Harry   What?

Cathy   Can you touch my face?

Harry   No.

He looks away from her.

A long time.

He looks at her.

He reaches over and very gently touches her face.

He holds his hand there. She touches his hand. She lets go.

He moves his hand away.

They look out over the horizon.

Cathy   Thank you.

Some more time.

The lights fade.

 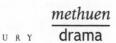

For a complete catalogue
of Bloomsbury Methuen Drama
titles write to:

Bloomsbury Methuen Drama
Bloomsbury Publishing Plc
50 Bedford Square
London WC1B 3DP

or you can visit our website at:
www.bloomsbury.com/drama